Hate Crimes

Other books in the Social Issues Firsthand series:

SOCIAL ISSUES
FIRSTHAND

Hate Crimes

Laurie Willis, Book Editor

GREENHAVEN PRESS

An imprint of Thomson Gale, a part of The Thomson Corporation

THOMSON

GALE

Detroit • New York • San Francisco • New Haven, Conn. • Waterville, Maine • London

Christine Nasso, *Publisher*
Elizabeth Des Chenes, *Managing Editor*

LIBRARY OF CONGRESS CATALOGING-IN-PUBLICATION DATA

Hate crimes / Laurie Willis, book editor.
  p. cm. -- (Social issues firsthand)
  Includes bibliographical references and index.
  ISBN-13: 978-0-7377-2889-7 (alk. paper)
  1. Hate crimes--United States. I. Willis, Laurie.
  HV6773.52.H367 2007
  364.15--dc22

                                            2006028623

ISBN-10: 0-7377-2889-2 (alk. paper)

Printed in the United States of America
10 9 8 7 6 5 4 3 2 1

Contents

Chapter 3: Taking Action Against Hate

Chapter 4: Hate Crimes and Genocide

Foreword

Social issues are often viewed in abstract terms. Pressing challenges such as poverty, homelessness, and addiction are viewed as problems to be defined and solved. Politicians, social scientists, and other experts engage in debates about the extent of the problems, their causes, and how best to remedy them. Often overlooked in these discussions is the human dimension of the issue. Behind every policy debate over poverty, homelessness, and substance abuse, for example, are real people struggling to make ends meet, to survive life on the streets, and to overcome addiction to drugs and alcohol. Their stories are ubiquitous and compelling. They are the stories of everyday people—perhaps your own family members or friends—and yet they rarely influence the debates taking place in state capitols, the national Congress, or the courts.

The disparity between the public debate and private experience of social issues is well illustrated by looking at the topic of poverty. Each year the United States Census Bureau establishes a poverty threshold. A household with an income below the threshold is defined as poor, while a household with an income above the threshold is considered able to live on a basic subsistence level. For example, in 2003 a family of two was considered poor if its income was less than $12,015; a family of four was defined as poor if its income was less than $18,810. Based on this system, the bureau estimates that 35.9 million Americans (12.5 percent of the population) lived below the poverty line in 2003, including 12.9 million children below the age of eighteen.

Commentators disagree about what these statistics mean. Social activists insist that the huge number of officially poor Americans translates into human suffering. Even many families that have incomes above the threshold, they maintain, are likely to be struggling to get by. Other commentators insist that the statistics exaggerate the problem of poverty in the United States. Compared to people in developing countries, they point out, most so-called poor families have a high quality of life. As stated by journalist Fidelis Iyebote, "Cars are owned by 70 percent of 'poor' households. . . . Color televisions belong to 97 percent of the 'poor' [and] videocassette recorders belong to nearly 75 percent. . . . Sixty-four percent have microwave ovens, half own a stereo system, and over a quarter possess an automatic dishwasher."

However, this debate over the poverty threshold and what it means is likely irrelevant to a person living in poverty. Simply put, poor people do not need the government to tell them whether they are poor. They can see it in the stack of bills they cannot pay. They are aware of it when they are forced to choose between paying rent or buying food for their children. They become painfully conscious of it when they lose their homes and are forced to live in their cars or on the streets. Indeed, the written stories of poor people define the meaning of poverty more vividly than a government bureaucracy could ever hope to. Narratives composed by the poor describe losing jobs due to injury or mental illness, depict horrific tales of childhood abuse and spousal violence, recount the loss of friends and family members. They evoke the slipping away of social supports and government assistance, the descent into substance abuse and addiction, the harsh realities of life on the streets. These are the perspectives on poverty that are too often omitted from discussions over the extent of the problem and how to solve it.

Greenhaven Press's Social Issues Firsthand series provides a forum for the often-overlooked human perspectives on society's most divisive topics of debate. Each volume focuses on one social issue and presents a collection of ten to sixteen narratives by those who have had personal involvement with the topic. Extra care has been taken to include a diverse range of perspectives. For example, in the volume on adoption, readers will find the stories of birth parents who have made an adoption plan, adoptive parents, and adoptees themselves. After exposure to these varied points of view, the reader will have a clearer understanding that adoption is an intense, emotional experience full of joyous highs and painful lows for all concerned.

The debate surrounding embryonic stem cell research illustrates the moral and ethical pressure that the public brings to bear on the scientific community. However, while nonexperts often criticize scientists for not considering the potential negative impact of their work, ironically the public's reaction against such discoveries can produce harmful results as well. For example, although the outcry against embryonic stem cell research in the United States has resulted in fewer embryos being destroyed, those with Parkinson's, such as actor Michael J. Fox, have argued that prohibiting the development of new stem cell lines ultimately will prevent a timely cure for the disease that is killing Fox and thousands of others.

Each book in the series contains several features that enhance its usefulness, including an in-depth introduction, an annotated table of contents, bibliographies for further research, a list of organizations to contact, and a thorough index. These elements—combined with the poignant voices of people touched by tragedy and triumph—make the Social Issues Firsthand series a valuable resource for research on today's topics of political discussion.

Introduction

Responding to Hate Crimes with Pleas for Tolerance

According to the United States House of Representatives, "the term 'hate crime' is a crime in which the defendant's conduct was motivated by hatred, bias, or prejudice, based on the actual or perceived race, color, religion, national origin, ethnicity, gender, or sexual orientation of another individual or group of individuals."[1] A hate crime victim, therefore, is not selected because he or she has provoked the anger or hatred of the perpetrator, but because of the perpetrator's prejudice against a group to which the victim belongs. Hate crimes range from acts of vandalism to murder, and many are intended to intimidate targeted groups and not merely specific victims. In spreading fear, hate crimes are usually successful because race, gender, sexual orientation, and religion are facets of personal identity as well as elements that bond people as part of a larger group.

The expected response to hate crime would be anger, hatred, and a desire for revenge. Indeed, many victims or victimized communities do react with these feelings. Some attempt to fight back by taking the law into their own hands, and others work toward the passing of legislation to punish the perpetrators. Given the serious and devastating nature of these crimes, it is striking, then, how often hate crimes produce reactions untainted by revenge. Rather than respond with hate to those who are hateful, some victims, their families, and their friends focus on teaching tolerance and promoting understanding. Their message is that the only means of overcoming hate crime is to eliminate the motivations and beliefs that breed hate crime.

Bringing People Together and Teaching Tolerance

One woman traumatized by a murderous hate crime was She-rialyn Byrdsong, the wife of Ricky Byrdsong, an African American basketball coach who was shot and killed near his home by a white supremacist in July 1999. Grieving the sense-lessness of her husband's death, Sherialyn created the Ricky Byrdsong Foundation, an organization with a mission "to ar-rest the growing epidemic of hate and violence in our society by and against our youth. By providing opportunities that broaden perspective, build character and instill a sense of pur-pose, the foundation promotes reconciliation and champions diversity."[2] The Byrdsong Foundation brings together youth from diverse ethnic backgrounds to discuss issues and form relationships with people different from themselves, so that they will grow up with tolerance and understanding.

Another organization formed in response to a supposed hate crime killing is the Matthew Shepard Foundation. Mat-thew Shepard was a twenty-one-year-old gay college student who was severely beaten in Laramie, Wyoming, by two men in 1998. His assailants, who accompanied Shepard out of a local gay bar, committed the assault and left Shepard tied to a fence where he died of his wounds five days later. Although Shepard's killers claim the murder was about drugs and money, the public and the gay community were initially con-vinced that Shepard was targeted because of his sexual orien-tation. Shepard's parents, who also believe that their son was murdered in a hate crime, established the Matthew Shepard Foundation in his memory. The mission of the organization is "to replace hate with understanding, compassion, and accep-tance."[3] Judy Shepard, Matthew's mother and the director of the foundation, believes her son's death is not a unique trag-edy in a nation so plagued by discrimination. She hopes that by promoting diversity and educating young people she is honoring Matthew's own beliefs about respecting the dignity of all people.

Outsiders Inspired to Get Involved

Matthew Shepard's death also inspired outsiders to get involved in telling the story of hate and hope in America. Moises Kaufman and members of the Tectonic Theater Project of New York City felt the incident was so important that the whole theater company traveled to Laramie, Wyoming, to interview the people of the town and get a sense of the community's reaction to Matthew's story. They wrote a play, *The Laramie Project*, which has been performed in schools and communities around the country. It was also adapted into a film for the HBO cable network. *The Laramie Project* uses the words of the community members as a mirror for the audience to examine their own prejudices. In an interview about *The Laramie Project*, Kaufman said:

> Most importantly, *The Laramie Project* tries to put us in touch with our common humanity. Past the issues, past the ideas, it tries to focus attention on how we are all different and how we are all the same. When Matthew's murder happened, the students at the high school in Laramie were really shaken by it. And I think this is an opportunity for students all around the country to meditate on what that meant, and on how they can take steps to prevent another Matthew Shepard from being murdered in their communities and in their schools.[4]

In 1993 the citizens of Billings, Montana, made a brave showing of their solidarity for those affected by hate crimes in the community. In that year the town was besieged by a sudden increase in racist literature and flyers, vandalism, and violence against Jews, Native Americans, and African Americans. As Hanukkah, a Jewish holiday, approached, vandals began throwing rocks through windows of homes displaying menorahs (candelabras), a symbol of the Jewish faith and of holiday celebration. Rather than resigning itself to the growing climate of hate, the community took a stand. More than ten thousand households, most of which were not Jewish, displayed paper menorahs in their windows to express their solidarity with the victims of the attacks. The *Not in Our Town* project began as a public television film documenting the story of how the residents of Billings joined together to resist hatred. Other communities have sponsored showings of the film combined with discussions, curriculum, and related events. The project has been so successful that sequels to the original film have been produced, featuring communities generating their own responses to hate.

Cutting Off the Chain of Hate

The common factor in all of these endeavors is the focus on recognizing prejudices, on acknowledging and accepting diversity, and building communities that respect the rights and integrity of all individuals. The creators of these programs believe that this type of education is the key to reducing the number of hate crimes. They also put a strong emphasis on working with youth. They view the prejudices underlying hate crime as learned behaviors that can be countered by education. Only by influencing future generations, these organizations maintain, can society arrest the motivations for hate crimes. Furthermore, these groups believe that spreading the message of tolerance builds community resistance to hate crimes and counters the fear and silent acceptance borne by those who are not directly targeted by hate crimes.

It is unfortunate that many such foundations form only after a hate-related tragedy has occurred. However, by educating young people, advocates of tolerance and diversity hope to end the chain of violence and destructive behaviors that make their organizations necessary. People such as Sherialyn Byrdsong and Judy Shepard preach the message of acceptance and respect so that the tragedy they experienced will not be visited upon other parents, spouses, and loved ones. It is a brave reaction to a heinous type of crime that is all too common in the world today.

Notes

1. *Hate Crimes Sentencing Enhancement Act of 1992*, HR 4797, 102nd Cong., 2nd sess.
2. Ricky Byrdsong Foundation. www.byrdsongfoundation.org.
3. Matthew Shepard Foundation. www.matthewshepard.org.
4. Quoted in *Time* Classroom: *The Laramie Project*, "Q&A Moises Kaufman." www.time.com.

CHAPTER 1

Messengers of Hate

The Recruitment Tactics of Skinheads

T.J. Leyden, interviewed by Vivienne Walt

When he was a teenager, T.J. Leyden was part of the punk rock scene. Older members of a neo-Nazi group called the Skinheads noticed that Leyden had a tendency towards violence, beating up on anyone who accidentally bumped him at punk concerts. He was recruited by the Skinheads and spent 15 years as a member of the Hammerskins of Southern California and other similar movements. It was not until he had children of his own that he decided it was time to get out. He changed his life and became a consultant for the Task Force Against Hate at the Simon Wiesenthal Center in Los Angeles.

In the following interview Leyden talks about his own recruitment by the Skinheads as well as his subsequent role as a recruiter himself. This interview took place a few days after Benjamin Nathaniel Smith, a former member of a racist organization called the World Church of the Creator (now known as the "Creativity Movement"), went on a shooting spree against Orthodox Jews, African Americans, and Asian Americans. Leyden refers to Smith several times in the interview. The interview was conducted by Vivienne Walt, a reporter who has been published in numerous news magazines.

When T.J. Leyden heard about Benjamin Nathaniel Smith's Fourth of July shooting spree against blacks, Asian-Americans and Orthodox Jews—which ended with Smith turning his gun on himself during a police chase—he was probably one of the few Americans who was not shocked. Nor was he perplexed that a young man like Smith—who grew up

T.J. Leyden, interviewed by Vivienne Walt, "American History Ex," Salon.com, July 8, 1999. This article first appeared in Salon.com, at http://www.salon.com. An online version remains in the Salon archives. Reprinted with permission.

in a comfortable Illinois suburb, attended elite public schools and was versed in Plato—would end up as a disciple of the World Church of the Creator, a racist organization.

At 33, Leyden has seen it all before. In fact, he has lived it: His life in violent neo-Nazi movements was launched at the age of 14, when he began punching out kids at punk rock concerts.

But unlike Smith's story, Leyden's is one of transformation. Four years ago, after watching his small son recoil in revulsion at the "niggers" on television, he quit the movement and his marriage to a fellow skinhead. Today, he is a full-time consultant to the Task Force Against Hate at the Simon Wiesenthal Center in Los Angeles, monitoring racist groups and, more importantly, trying to extract young men and women from them. In fact, while Smith was prowling the suburbs of Chicago and Bloomington, Ind., last weekend [July 3–4, 1999] Leyden was at a rally of skinheads in Las Vegas—this time as an enemy within their midst, hoping to reach some youth before they end up on a rampage like Smith.

In the wake of the weekend's violence, Leyden spoke to Salon Mothers Who Think about the vulnerability of youth, what he learned from his own children and his dealings with Benjamin Smith's mentor, Matthew Hale, the head of the World Church of the Creator.

Vivienne Walt: What kind of person is Matthew Hale?

T.J. Leyden: I've never met him, but I used to talk to him on the phone when we were organizing concerts and festivals. We'd network. He's smart, a good talker and a great propagandist. He's only 29. He knows how to manipulate the whole thing, like saying he's a white separatist, not a white supremacist. That's a lie. They believe in RAHOWA—the Race Holy War—that you have to cleanse the world of all non-Aryans. The COTC, as they call it, is really starting to grow over the last couple of years, they're in 35 cities now. That's partly because of Matt.

Walt: What effect will last weekend's events have on his movement?

Leyden: In one way, it's bad for Matt because it's brought to light a lot of stuff that he'd preferred not to have come to light. But in other ways, it's good: There will be kids who say, "This group is actually doing something, they're not just big talk." And they'll join. That's what Matt wants, and that's what he'll get. In some way, Benjamin Smith will become a martyr.

Walt: You spent 15 years in some of the most violent skinhead movements, mostly the Hammerskins of Southern California. Didn't the violence ever bother you?

Leyden: When I first got involved, I didn't really like the violence. But after a while, nah, it didn't bother me at all. It was just something we did: violence, fighting. At first, we wouldn't beat up a lot of people; we'd just recruit more and more kids. Then we started getting into violence. We would beat up white kids in the neighborhood who weren't involved, or blacks and Latinos who weren't supposed to be there. We used to call it a bonus if we got blacks and Latinos—if they came into our neighborhood, they'd get beaten up.

One kid that we fought—he was white—we cracked his ribs, separated his shoulder, kicked four of his teeth out and broke his jaw. And I broke the kid's thumb; it shattered when I kicked it. Supposedly he tripped a skinhead girl—or that's what she said. I don't know if he did. He was in the wrong place at the wrong time.

Walt: How does it happen that someone like you, a good kid from a good neighborhood, winds up a violent racist?

Leyden: Benjamin Smith grew up like I did: nice neighborhood, good family, parents who supposedly loved him and cared about him even though they didn't support his racism. Neither did my parents.

I was from an upper-middle-class neighborhood in Fontana, Calif., part of the Inland Empire. All my friends were white, everyone at school was white. My dad ran his own business installing telephones, and he made really good money. My mom worked her way up working for San Bernardino County. We weren't the richest kids in town, but if we wanted something we knew we were going to get it. I got involved after my parents got divorced. My mom and dad didn't know what was going on—they were going through this divorce and they just kind of lost track of what me and my brothers were doing. My brothers went the opposite way—one's a cop.

Walt: Who recruited you?

Leyden: First I got involved in the punk rock scene, then I started being a bit more violent than my friends. If someone bumped me at a concert, I'd beat on them. The older guys saw this and liked it and asked me to hang out with them.

Back then, the skins were bi-racial, mostly white and Latino. It was only in 1981 that they got racist. The skins split up into different factions. I was in the racist faction—the White Tribe, we called ourselves; then American Firm and Hammerskins on the West Coast. We were only about 35 kids. I started getting into a lot of trouble and had a couple of drunk driving convictions and assault charges.

Walt: A lot of kids survive divorce, and worse, and don't become racists. What makes the recruitment into these organizations so successful?

Leyden: Everybody is vulnerable at a certain point in their lives, and you look for people with that kind of vulnerability. Recruitment is everything in these organizations. There is no certain kind of person who gets into these movements—there are people from all walks of life.

A lot of them are just bored. Really bored. They go home and get on the Internet. The Internet has really, really changed things. The movements have flooded the Internet with racist sites. There are probably over 2,000 now. We find new ones all the time at the [Simon Wiesenthal] Center. So if a kid is unsupervised, it's easy pickings. And mom and dad don't want to talk about race, because race is a nasty subject.

You start listening to people saying this group is scum and that group is scum. You don't have the facts. You're young, you don't care about the facts, you don't take time to check things. It just somehow fits your description of the world, why this country is such a mess—the blacks and Asians are to blame, the Jews control the banks and so on.

This is what I try to tell parents now: The [Ku Klux] Klan isn't trying to recruit blacks and Latinos, they're trying to recruit your son and daughter. Most skinheads don't come from the poor part of town.

Walt: Doesn't cracking down on racist activists stop them?

Leyden: Well, I've been in jail a lot. How many times? Don't know—at least 12 times in five states between 1987 and 1995. Actually, jail didn't bother me. It was a country club after a while, once I knew the game I knew the ins and outs. It's not nice, but it's not hardcore. Usually you have associates in there and you can work things out inside.

I finally saw I was going to do some real serious damage to someone and go to jail for a really long time. So I had to leave. I joined the Marines. They accepted me because I had no felonies on my record. I was a race recruiter in the Marines, in Hawaii—I passed out literature and got people to join the Hammerskins. I also started working with the Nation of Islam in the Marines, to start race riots, so we could both recruit people. We'd start as many as we could, so it was easier for us to recruit them. People thought they were just fighting each other, but in reality, we were pulling all the strings.

Walt: What finally made you leave the racist movement?

Leyden: I got out of the Marines in 1990 and married a girl from Texas I'd been writing to. We married 14 days after we met. She was racist, I was racist and we wanted kids. We had two sons and I decided I wasn't going to be a street soldier anymore. I had a family now—I'd get guys like Benjamin Smith to do my dirty work for me. So I became a race recruiter. But then my kids started doing racist things, thinking it was really cool. They saw TV shows with someone black and say, "Turn it off, we can't watch shows with niggers on"— little things like that. It's one thing *you* doing these things, but when you see your kids doing it . . . I just turned it off. Nicole and I got divorced. The boys are 5 and 8 now; they live half with me, half with her. Without my boys, I'm sure I'd be in prison somewhere.

Walt: When the movie "American History X" came out last year [1998], a lot of reviewers thought it was ridiculous that a racist could go through a total transformation. In fact, it seems to be your story.

Leyden: A couple of the screenwriters came to hear me speak before the movie was made, but I don't know if I'm the inspiration. Things happen to transform people—for this kid [in the film], it was jail. The movie was really accurate, as close as Hollywood's gotten to portraying the race movement. Perhaps the transformation was very cut and dry, but you have only so much time in a movie.

Walt: You've turned your own transformation into a full-time campaign. What do you do for the Simon Wiesenthal Center?

Leyden: I travel around a lot, talking at schools, colleges, churches, synagogues, to anyone who'll listen to me. I talk to law enforcement people probably on a daily basis.

I talk to racist kids. I do it by becoming their friend, telling them they can learn from my mistakes. Of course I get called all sorts of nice little names. I've been called a "race traitor" by every movement out there. I've got 10 kids out of the racist movements over three years. That may not be a lot, but it's a start. You get a couple of kids out and you're stopping them from recruiting more.

Walt: Ten kids in three years! But the Internet, you say, could be drawing in hundreds of them. How do you ever get ahead of the curve?

Leyden: I wish I had the answer to that; it's an incredibly difficult question. You have to work out everything very slowly. I tell parents they have to talk to their kids about race. We keep an eye on these groups and we monitor certain days: Hitler's birthday [April 20, the day of the Columbine school massacre]; Nov. 9, Kristelnacht [when Nazis rioted against Jews just prior to World War II]; and Dec. 8, the day Robert Jay Matthews [the leader of the white separatist organization called the Order Bruder Schweigen] was killed in a firefight with the feds in Idaho in 1984. July 4 is Day of Revolution—I was in Vegas not celebrating Independence Day but monitoring white supremacists. There are plenty of Benjamin Smiths still out there.

Warning Against the Sin of Homosexuality

Fred Phelps Sr.

The Reverend Fred Phelps Sr. established the Westboro Baptist Church (WBC) in Topeka, Kansas, in 1955. Believing homosexuality is condemned by God, Phelps believes homosexuals are a danger to the survival of America. He considers it his responsibility to warn people of this danger. In the following narrative, Phelps describes the picketing campaign his church staged in Topeka's Gage Park, which he asserted was frequented by homosexuals. Phelps and members of his congregation began staging daily sidewalk demonstrations at the park in 1991, carrying signs proclaiming "GOD HATES FAGS" and similar messages. Since the campaign at Gage Park, WBC demonstrators have picketed against homosexuality throughout the United States and in several other countries. According to Phelps, they have participated in over 20,000 demonstrations. The demonstrators have received considerable media attention for picketing gay-pride parades, the funerals of homosexuals, and other events.

On May 24, 1954 the Lord brought my wife and me to Topeka. . . .

In November 1955 the first worship service was held of the Westboro Baptist Church. With a strong heart, and an uncertainty about the future, I began preaching the doctrines of grace, as they were unfolded to me by God. Those powerful and precious doctrines have sustained us through all these years. We had the promise that the gates of hell would not prevail against this little church. From that day, we have maintained a conspicuous testimony of truth in an increasingly perverse generation, earnestly contending for the faith that was once delivered. . . .

Fred Phelps Sr., "A Message to Topeka from Fred Phelps: How It All Began," *Topeka Capital-Journal Online*. Reproduced by permission.

How the Picketing Started

Eleven years ago we began our picket ministry, opposing the filth of homosexuality. Recall how it started. We grew weary of our young men being accosted at Gage Park, in the light of day, by militant homosexuals. Naively, we approached the city officials, thinking surely if they knew they would stop it. What we did not reckon is the exponential rate at which this nation, this state, this city, and all of the so-called leaders, had deeply corrupted themselves. The abominations that occur on a routine basis in this country today are shocking. No thought is given to being chaste. All thought and dialogue evolves around serving the flesh.

Rather than do the decent thing—clean up the park—the government, with one voice, sharply criticized us, and refused to act. Today we understand how weak they had become. Today we understand the enormous pressure brought to bear by depraved homosexuals, lying false prophets, and the media. It will stand as an eternal shrine of shame to the leaders of this city that they gave in to that pressure, and left the matter of cleaning up that park in our hands.

The national directory that lists this park as a place to cruise for anonymous fag sex, today says that you do so at your own risk. When we started, the directory said fags seeking sex at the park enjoyed the protection of law enforcement while engaging in their filth in the bushes. And there is not an enlightened soul the world over who doesn't equate Gage Park with homosexuality, thanks to our ministry shining a light on that fact.

We learned with time that none of the 400+ churches in this area would lift a hand about this disgrace. Worse, the large, mainstream churches enable and support it. Strong Bible metaphors come to mind watching these houses of idolatry, these dog kennels, these pigsties, join forces and use every conceivable strategy to try and stop us. What they failed to calculate was the simple fact that he who holds the Key to

David opens doors of utterance, and no man can shut them. They also failed to account for the fact that every prophet of God who has lived has cried against these altars. That's our job, and we will do it until these churches get right with God, or Christ returns, whichever comes first. The good money is on Christ returning first. . . .

What Is the Purpose of Picketing?

Let me further touch on our purpose. We don't strive to change your hearts or minds. For God alone controls the hearts of man. Even if we wanted to, we couldn't make you believe the truth. In fact, the scriptures are full of verses telling us you will not believe our report. God has reserved to himself only a remnant. No man can come to Christ except the Father who sent Christ draw that man. These are the words of Christ. Christ also said, just before he was murdered, that he did not pray for the whole world, but only those God gave him out of the world.

Every person who is predestined for hell will remain in darkness. Christ told the apostles that he spoke in fables so the blind would not understand. Scores of verses bespeak God's power and plan to blind the eyes, harden the hearts, stop up the ears, and preserve in iniquity, those whom he does not love. To understand God's love, says Malachi in Chapter 1, you have to understand God's hate. To understand the richness of his glory in carving out a remnant for salvation and grace, you have to understand the power of his glory in reserving the rest for darkness.

If God has blinded you by a divine stroke, we won't open your eyes. Our purpose is to publish. Our job is to warn you to flee the wrath to come. We've warned you, and you've responded with deliberate rebellion and anger. The citizens of Sodom will rise up in testimony against Topeka. Sodom was destroyed for embracing and institutionalizing sexual perversion. (Don't waste our time pretending the sin of Sodom was discourtesy. The definition of sodomy is anal copulation, not impoliteness.) If Topeka does not receive the same measure of punishment Sodom received, and more, the citizens of ancient Sodom will have a cause. For their deeds could not be worse than Topeka's.

Not one soul who ever spent more than a day in Topeka will be able to claim he was not warned. I pity to think what kind of trouble you are in if you've lived here all through these years, cursing us without measure, with a full understanding of our message. You will be absolutely without excuse. Your blood will not be on our hands. And we will have some rich and exciting testimony to give against you. Along with the multitude of angels who have compassed us about, holding us up, and bearing witness to all you have done.

This Nation Is Doomed

We are satisfied that like old Israel this nation is doomed. Jeremiah was told by God to go tell the children of Israel that it was all over. That he was going to destroy them for their many grievous sins against him. They were stiff-necked, proud, and unrepentant. Jeremiah, being a tenderhearted soul (like all God's people), went back to God three times, to pray for the people. God told him to stop praying! God told him even if Moses and Samuel stood before him, his mind could not go toward the children of Israel. He told Jeremiah to cast them out of his sight. Jeremiah warned them. They refused to repent. And they were destroyed.

There is a point of no return with God. You cannot raise your middle finger toward God year in and out without serious consequences. It is too late for this city. It is too late for this state. It is too late for America. Any preacher who tells you otherwise is lying! Worse, he (or God forbid, she) is doing so for filthy lucre and to justify his own sins. You are in a world of trouble Topeka! . . .

God Doesn't Love an Impenitent Homosexual

One more thought about the militant homosexuals who are the focus of the dialogue. (Remember, we didn't make them the front burner moral issue in America today. They did. They are driven to force every human to call them holy. Once they're on the front page, however, we're going to bring the Bible perspective to the matter. Including when they get on the front page by some high-profile death that they convert into a platform for their cause.)

False religionists love to offer God's love to these creatures. The God-awful lie behind that offer, which they have no business making, is that forgiveness from God is available for the impenitent. Everyone knows better. But they seize that lie and scream it at us every day.

There is no forgiveness without repentance. There is no repentance without quitting the sin. You cannot march in "Gay Pride" parades, and then claim that God loves you. Impenitent hard sinners have no inheritance in heaven.

Topeka's Reaction

It is most remarkable watching Topeka react to this message. After all these years, you still cuss, spit, scream, raise your middle finger, swerve your vehicles at us, repeat the most absurd lies about God, and hate us. Isn't that ironic. You hate us. While you insist that we not hate. (Pretending you don't understand this is God's—not man's—hate we're talking about.) "Hatemonger!" you bellow, while you hate God and hate our message down to your toenails.

Why do you suppose that seemingly rational people by their majority react in such anger? Even after seeing these words literally thousands of times? The answer is simple. Because you know it's true. Every human is born with knowledge of God and his attributes. You know that God has attributes called anger, wrath, hate and vengeance. You know that on a certain day you will be called before God the Sovereign and be held to an account for your words and deeds in the flesh. You know the Great White Throne awaits all of us, and that in the end, every knee shall bow and every tongue shall confess and call him Lord.

Promoting the White Supremacist Worldview

Matthew Hale, interviewed by Matt Sharkey

Matthew Hale has been a leader in a number of white suprema-cist organizations, beginning with the National Socialist White Americans' Party, which he founded in 1992. In 1999, at the age of 28, Hale was the "Pontifex Maximus" of the World Church of the Creator (WCOTC), later to be known as the "Creativity Movement." This organization advocates a "White Religion" called "Creativity."

In July 1999, Benjamin Nathaniel Smith, a former member of the World Church of the Creator, went on a shooting spree, targeting Orthodox Jews, African Americans, and Asian Ameri-cans. He killed two men and wounded seven others, then took his own life. In the following interview with staff writer Matt Sharkey of Generator 21: The World's Magazine, *Matthew Hale talks about Smith's relationship to the WCOTC, calling him "a martyr for free speech" because of the publicity for the move-ment which resulted from Smith's actions. Hale also talks about the ideology behind the White Supremacist movement, giving his justifications for why the white race should remain separate from other races, which he considers to be inferior.*

G21: . . . I would like to talk about Benjamin Smith, if you don't mind.

Matthew Hale: Sure.

G21: The letter you received was mailed on the Friday of the first shooting [July 2, 1999], and in it he formally renounced his membership in the church. I'm wondering why, if he had left the church in April, he felt it necessary to do that at that point.

Matthew Hale, interviewed by Matt Sharkey, "The Matt Hale Interview," *Generator 21: The World's Magazine*, August 1–8, 1999. Reproduced by permission.

Hale: It's obvious now that he wanted to make sure that the world knew, as much as they don't want to know, that he was responsible for his own actions. I certainly think that is the reason he wrote that letter. He wanted to make sure that people realized that, no, he was not sent out to do what he did, and that the church is indeed a legal organization.

G21: That is the language used in the letter. He didn't speak to you about this at all?

Hale: Not at all. . . .

G21: Let's backtrack a bit. You met Benjamin Smith when?

Hale: I met him in August of last year.

G21: Of 1998.

Hale: Yes.

G21: And yet he was named "Creator of the Year" for 1998.

Hale: That's right. He did a very fine job the last four, five months of the year—in fact, probably the last six months of the year—passing out literature. But he did pass out the literature before I'd met him. . . .

Relationship with Smith

G21: You told the FBI that Smith was a friend. You also told them that you were unaware of Smith's plot. Yet, you met with him ten days before the shootings, at a restaurant, weeks after he'd withdrawn seventeen thousand dollars from his bank accounts. There was no mention of his plan?

Hale: He never mentioned [his plans] to me at all. Obviously, it would not be in my interests, either as a citizen of this country or as a person trying to get a law license, to encourage anybody to commit a crime. Certainly, if he'd told me anything about this, if he'd said, "Pontifex"—that's what he always called me, out of respect—"Pontifex, I'm thinking about killing people," I'd have said, "Brother, don't do it." He obviously didn't tell me about this because he wanted to protect me.

G21: Yet, when the FBI questioned you, you said that on the evening of 3 July, when news reports revealed the model and color of the shooter's car, you suspected that it was Smith.

Hale: Not really. I didn't really suspect it. I just thought that it could be him because he had a car like that. But as I also said to the FBI, the sketch didn't look like him at all. The sketch being shown all over the television looked as much like him as I look like him.

G21: You told them, and the quote is from the [Chicago] *Tribune* reporters who were present, "When you haven't heard from a friend you heard was going to the Chicago suburbs and you usually talk to him every other day or so, and the suspect is driving a light blue Ford Taurus, my dad and I both kind of wondered."

Hale: That's accurate.

G21: So you had your suspicions, at least.

Hale: I hate to go into semantics, but what does "suspicion" or "suspect" mean? If you had a blue Taurus and somebody committed a crime two states away, I might think of you. That doesn't mean I suspect you.

G21: But specifically a hate-crime, in fitting with the ideology of the church and Benjamin Smith personally, did not strike you as odd or something that should be reported?

Hale: I didn't think it should be reported. I certainly did not think I had any evidence that it was him, so I didn't think it would be appropriate.

G21: You knew he was going to Chicago, yes?

Hale: I didn't know where he was going to pass out the literature. He said the Chicago suburbs. That's all I knew.

G21: But then it was two cities where he attended college.

Hale: Wait a minute. By Saturday, he hadn't even gone to Bloomington, Indiana, yet. The U of I thing, I don't even know if I knew about it at that point. It's not like I was riveted to the television while this was going on. I certainly wasn't. I had the newspaper, I turned on the Headline News, and I went about my business.

G21: He left the church in April.

Hale: He said April, I thought it was May.

G21: And you received his card on 7 July.

Hale: Yes, I think so.

G21: The card specifically absolved you of guilt. You specifically.

Hale: Sure. He was a friend of mine. He obviously wanted people to know the truth.

G21: At the point he was apprehended, shot himself—

Hale: I hope that's what happened. I'm going to be making a move to get a copy of the autopsy report to make sure. I have to say the media sure has jumped on this suicide business. Kind of strange to shoot one's self three times to commit suicide. I'd hoped the media would be a bit more primed than that.

G21: You suspect the police?

Hale: It's possible, sure. . . .

Explaining the "Facts"

G21: What was the literature Smith was to distribute during the Fourth of July weekend?

Hale: I presume it was the "Facts". I didn't see his trunk. This is hard to remember. It was really so non-eventful. I meet so many people, I talk to so many people, and so many people get literature. I seem to recall he was going to pass out the "Facts".

G21: Can you elaborate on what the "Facts" is?

Hale: The "Facts" is basically an objective discussion of a number of items that people probably don't know about, including the Jewish Talmud. The teachings in there are very hostile to non-Jews. The facts about Jewish control of media, how they have a disproportionate amount of control. Facts about the kosher food tax, which are foods taxed to be blessed by a rabbi. Facts about our founding fathers and their statements about the Jews, including George Washington and Benjamin Franklin. Facts about crime, the Black disproportionate amount of it being committed. Immigration facts. Things of that nature.

G21: That these statements don't stand up to the facts of history doesn't seem to deter your publication of them in your literature.

Hale: Throughout history, history has changed. For example, the Encyclopedia Britannica used to talk about Blacks having smaller and less developed brains. Just because it doesn't say that anymore doesn't mean it's not still true.

G21: But it *isn't* true.

Hale: It is true.

Racial Differences

G21: According to what study?

Hale: Let's just do this. Let's get a couple cadavers and let's examine them. I'd be more than happy to do that. As much as I'm not a guy for blood and guts, I'd be more than happy to demonstrate this.

G21: Most studies show that the difference was based on subjective selection.

Hale: That's just propaganda. I know this is hard for you to understand. I've been researching this and studying this since I was twelve years old. Most people, I don't blame them for coming into this and saying, gee whiz, there's a conspiracy around every corner, you guys are just trying to justify your beliefs with faulty science and history. I don't blame people for thinking that. You probably think that as well. But the fact of the matter is that when you have something that walks like a duck, talks like a duck, swims like a duck, it probably is a duck. And when you have a situation where the Jews have been hated throughout history, there must be a reason. It just doesn't make any sense to say that it was just scapegoating or anything like that. Our ancestors hated them and hated them for a reason. They hated them because they are manipulators, they are controllers of economies and governments. People get fed up with that.

G21: Other than existing prejudice, what evidence is there to justify this?

Hale: I can give you a very good example. Throughout the centuries, Jews were accused and convicted of ritual murder. They did this throughout Europe, Germany, France, Italy, Russia, Austria, probably other countries. They would kidnap white kids and sacrifice them to Yahweh. Now, these were recorded events. This isn't something that was cast about out of thin air.

As far as other historical events, there's Communism. Comminism was founded by Karl Marx. What was his real name? Mortecai Levy. Who was Trotsky? Lev Bronstein. Who was Friedrich Engels? A half Jew. Three hundred eleven out of the first three hundred eighty-four members of the Politburo of the Soviet Union were Jews.

G21: And Mao Tse-tung? Stalin?

Hale: Stalin was said to be one-quarter, but there's dispute about that. He did marry a Jew. Certainly there have been non-Jewish communists, but I'm saying that the whole idea originated from the Jews. They have come up with everything bad in the world. Hitler was right about that. Hitler said in *Mein Kampf*, "Is there any filth or duplicity without at least one Jew involved?"

G21: You can't deny that white people throughout history have been responsible for many atrocities.

Hale: Certainly. But they're white people, and that's the thing. We look at it this way. There are plenty of bad apples on the white racial tree. Of course. But it's still our tree. Let the Jews take care of their tree and the Blacks take care of theirs, the Orientals take care of theirs, Arabs take care of theirs. We'll take care of our own.

Whites Need to Remain a Distinct Biological Entity

G21: You're saying, then, that the white race is no better than any other.

Hale: As far as good and bad, right. I mean, there are plenty of bad whites, but we're trying to create an all-white society because that's the only way our race can ultimately survive. The streets are telling us that. You see white women with blacks—white *men* with blacks, now—and other races mixing. We cannot survive as a distinct biological entity unless we are separate.

G21: But what is the importance of surviving as a "distinct biological entity"? How can you even grant that whites are a distinct biological entity?

Hale: How? Our eyes. There's a tremendous physical difference between whites and non-whites. There are two hundred genetic differences between whites and blacks. Everything from hair to sweat glands to eyes to mucous membranes to brain differences to running ability, jumping ability, fingerprints, blood types. All kinds of differences.

G21: The studies say that only 6% of genes contribute to racial differences, but even if the case is as extreme as you make it sound, why is that an insidious threat?

Hale: In nature, all creatures breed only with their own kind. Only when domesticated do creatures breed outside their own kind. So if which to remain true to the laws of nature, as we believe we should as human beings, we have to recognize this. And of course, we submit that whites mixing with other races destroys the quality of our people. If you take a white person and breed them with blacks, you'll have a medium grade as far as intelligence, and you'll also have a very confused individual without any solid racial background. I've even talked to people of mixed blood before, and they've admitted to me, "I don't have any real identity, I don't know what I am. I sometimes side with the black side, sometimes with the whites." It's really unfortunate.

G21: I'd submit that it's unfortunate that he'd have to choose between siding with a black side or a white side, but regardless, aren't we talking about humans?

Hale: Using that word is a value judgement, of sorts. Once again, I go back to nature. That's what we base our teachings on. In nature, you don't find black ants and red ants hitting it off. In fact, you find bitter enemies among them. You don't find black bears and grizzly bears co-mingling or interbreeding. That's why the non-whites are our enemies. They are rivals. Certainly, if they were rabbits or something, it wouldn't be much of a problem.

G21: But we're not talking about animals.

Hale: But we *are* animals. That's the thing. We don't accept this idea that just because we can think and speak and walk on two legs that we are not bound by nature's laws. We are.

White Supremacy As a Religion

G21: Why should a relatively insignificant difference within a species influence politics?

Hale: This isn't about politics. That's why we have a church, why I have forsaken politics. At one time, I used to consider myself a politician of sorts. I ran for city council, got fourteen percent of the vote four years ago. But this isn't about politics. This is about deciding what are our supreme values. We believe that everything that we appreciate in this world, whether it's technology, whether it's culture, whether it's civilization itself, is dependent on keeping the white race intact, and keeping it white. The other races have not created worthwhile cultures and technology and civilizations. They have only copied from us, at best, and destroyed us.

G21: Doesn't this contradict your statement that the Jewish race is in control?

Hale: The problem is that white people, as intelligent as they are, as creative as they are, are misdirecting their intelligence and creativity toward the betterment of the non-white races. That's the problem. Heck, the Jews are the most racist people on earth. What one Jew believes, they all believe. In fact, we look to the Jews, in some ways, for influence, as far as how a people that small, that insignificant in numbers, can become masters of the earth. They did it by having a racial religion, by being intolerant of others, by having a creed that was very exclusive.

G21: The same thing could be said of many religions.

Hale: I don't think so. If you read the New Testament, you don't read about white people smiling and killing other races. If you read our religion—which most people haven't. Once again, the problem is that they don't actually read our books. They like to talk about them, but they won't read them. You won't find any passages about us celebrating the non-whites being destroyed or anything else. One thing I'd really challenge you to do is read our first book. I'm trying to give the nutshell version of it, but it really doesn't do it complete justice. Ben Klassan spent five hundred pages detailing everything that I've said about nature and how we are bound by her laws, and that's why we have to do what we're doing here. I'd really encourage you to read it if you have the time.

G21: I've read the sections on your website, in research for this interview, and I have to say that what I see there is no different from what you are accusing other races of doing.

Hale: It's like this. We have to have a racially-exclusive religion if we're going to survive. That's the bottom line. We look at everything toward the end result. The end does justify the means, unquestionably. If the end is white survival, then the means are justified.

G21: But you'll agree that the majority of whites don't support your views.

Hale: I think they do in a lot of ways. For example, and this is a hypothetical I've used many a time, if white people could snap their fingers and the non-whites would disappear, I guarantee you ninety percent of the white race would snap their fingers. The problem is not that they disagree so much, it's just that they're lazy, and they won't do anything about it. The people sit in their easy chair—and I happen to be sitting in one right now, but I think I have good reason—they sit in their easy chair, and they nod their heads when they see us on television or get our flyer, etc., but they don't do anything. That's the problem.

Benjamin Smith Is a Martyr

G21: As for Ben Smith's actions, you have spoken out against the acts but not the ideology behind them. He did specifically target ethnic minorities.

Hale: It's true that if he'd shot white people, I'd denounce him.

G21: But you don't denounce him.

Hale: I don't denounce him.

G21: Is he considered a martyr of the church?

Hale: He is considered a martyr for free speech, because I think the reason that he did this is because of the persecution that he faced—and I faced—for simply exercising religious freedoms.

G21: The incident has gone a long way toward publicizing not only the church but you specifically. In that respect, this would be a boon for you.

Hale: And maybe that's what he wanted. Maybe he lost his life to make us a household name. As I've said on some of the stations, I have nothing but good things to say about Ben Smith. I have nothing bad to say about the man.

The Neo-Nazi Lifestyle

Tom Metzger, interviewed by Katia Dunn

In the following article Katia Dunn interviews white supremacist and leader of the White Aryan Nation, Tom Metzger. In this interview Metzger discusses his views on racism, recruitment strategy, and his vision and goals for the United States. The interview with Metzger coincided with his return to Portland to speak at a neo-Nazi event. Previously he had been in Portland, Oregon, following the murder of an Ethiopian man, Mulugeta Seraw, in 1988. Seraw was killed by white supremacists and Metzger was found guilty of training the killers and ordered to pay $12 million for his involvement in the hate crime. Katia Dunn is a journalist who has worked for the Portland Mercury *and National Public Radio.*

Katia Dunn: Are you a racist?

Tom Metzger: Yes, but I believe black people should be racist too. I think there's honor in protecting our neighborhood, your family, and, similarly, your race.

How do you gain supporters for your movement? Do you find them or do they find you?

First of all, we're not a membership organization. Membership organizations are easy targets for federal and state scrutiny. Instead, we work with voluntary associates, and because of that, I really have no idea how many people are involved. But they definitely come to us.

Like WAR [White Aryan Resistance], environmentalists in Portland are concerned about FBI scrutiny. They actually seem to share your general distrust of government. Any thoughts on this?

Tom Metzger, interviewed by Katia Dunn, "Straight from the Neo-Nazi's Mouth," *The Portland Mercury*, December 6–12, 2001. Reproduced by permission.

We have a lot of supporters from the environmental movement, because the two aren't that far apart. Open borders means more consumption of living space. With hundreds of thousands of Mexicans coming across the border, the biggest environmental problem is immigration. I have predicted for years that the environmental struggle and the racist struggle will come together. They have been running parallel for quite awhile, but are starting to blend together now.

Is there a common type of person who joins your movement?

It's very difficult to profile them [the people involved], because they come from all walks of life. A lot of them are professionals like us because they can operate covertly without worrying about losing their job—you never know who's working next to you. In fact, we recommend that people should play the "devil's advocate"; the office liberal. We've heard from people in the military, students, professors; in fact. I don't even know who's involved.

Recruitment and Goals

Is Portland a particularly good area to recruit in?

I don't think we have a lot of influence in Portland or Seattle. These areas are the poorest areas to recruit in because they haven't been subjected to integrated areas. Miami, San Francisco, LA those areas are more integrated and more separatist.

You haven't been in Portland for nearly a decade, since the death of Mulugeta Seraw [an Ethiopian man killed in 1988 in Portland; Metzger was found guilty of training the men who killed Seraw].

That was a total legal lynching. At this point, if I had actually done what they said I'd did, I'd say 'Yeah I did it.' But I didn't do it. I was dealing with a hysteria that was put together by elements in Portland, including the mayor. I will never forget the way I was treated in Portland. I'm not a Christian, but there's one saying in the Bible that says, "if there's one good man in the city, than you can spare the city." And there was one man in Portland who didn't believe the lies. I spared Portland for that man, euphemistically speaking. I think Portland is full of self-hating whites; people who will promote any person of color before promoting themselves.

If we were to abolish the present form of government, what would be a good replacement?

I support any kind of government that works well for the white person. In many ways, I'm quite libertarian. I believe that if you have a white homeland, within that homeland, freedom should be nationalized. If people want to smoke pot, fine. I would eliminate the drug war immediately, and that would release about two-thirds of all prisoners. Most of the people in jail are in on drugs, which aren't violent crimes. When the government says that by having a bag of marijuana, you have to go to jail, you have a police state. And this country is becoming a police state. I think a lot of people would agree with me there.

What's your ultimate goal?

Well, we'd just like to have North America. Other races, they can have all the other countries. We just want them out of ours.

Recruiting Hate in Prison

Mike Lando, interviewed by Sarah Childress

In the following article Sarah Childress interviews Mikey Lando, a fifty-six year old man who joined the white supremacist group Aryan Brotherhood while serving a prison term for armed robbery. In the interview Lando describes how he joined the Aryan Brotherhood, how to survive in the group, and the relationship between the Aryan Brotherhood and other white supremacist groups and prison gangs. Sarah Childress is a writer for Newsweek.

Newsweek: *How did you get involved in the gang?*

Mikey Lando: I don't like the word 'gang.' It's . . . a club, a crew. I've been a member since 1984. It's a part of survival there [in prison]. You've got to be part of something or you're dead. Either the AB [Aryan Brotherhood], or the Black Guerilla Family, or the Mexican Mafia or you're dead. You gotta join something. I was chosen to be in the AB and I was protected by the AB, and when I got out I joined the Aryan Nations [a white supremacy group].

How did you first become a member?

I didn't choose them—they chose me. They just liked my demeanor, they liked my jokes. I was buffed up anyway, physically. They approached me, and said you're one of us now, whether you like it or not. It's blood in, blood out.

That's an AB motto. What does it mean?

It's so hard, because it's . . . [*Sighs.*] It's just part of life. If you're out, you're dead. If you're in, you survive. I'm not proud of them, of what I've done in my life, in prison, what I've had to do for them. If you don't do for them what they

Mike Lando, interviewed by Sarah Childress, "Interview with a Member of the Aryan Brotherhood," *Newsweek*, February 5, 2006. All rights reserved. Reprinted by permission.

want you to do then you're dead. [B]ut I survived. And I got a color f—king TV. Out of all I've done in my life for the Aryan Brotherhood, I got a brand new color TV, and I've got my life.

Survival in the Gang

What did you have to do for them?

I got hold of shanks, drugs. Heroin. Once they brought in meth. It was p2p. Of course they wanted their cut, and I gave 'em their third when I brought in my issue. It tore 'em up! They said, "Mikey, that's your gig now." It was so strong. Of course they wanted their issue. They wanted their issue of anything. That's how I lived for my 17 years, whether I had to hide their shanks or hide their drugs or whatever, that's how I survived.

The AB started as a white power group—is it still that way?

Of course it's a white power group. [But] it's not necessarily . . . I've often said, if a n---er had heroin, he could join the Aryan Brotherhood. But they're so tight, if you screw up you're dead. They'd throw you off the third tier—after they set you on fire.

What's it like to be in that situation? Were you afraid?

Every time the cell door opens in the morning and you go to chow you're afraid. The only time you're not afraid is when the cell door closes. You're always afraid. . . . I'm the only one that made it out okay. I straightened out my life. I think I'm the only one that has been successful in life. When I got out I was all f—ked up in my head. You've done so much time you're just screwed up. But I made out okay, through family and friends. I got a lovely place to live and I don't bother nobody.

What do you think about the trial in California?

Puh! That ain't the big deal . . . Yeah, yeah, yeah, I know all those guys who got indictments in California. [*Laughs.*] You're never going to cripple the AB. If you kill one, there's going to be three more in its place.

Relationship with Other Gangs

The AB's membership stays small because they're so careful about who they let in. But they get other groups to work for them.

In California, you got the AB and another club that's even bigger, which is called the . . . what's them little bastards' names? The Nazi Low Riders [NLR]. They're an even bigger group as far as members go. They're the youngsters, and they're just as treacherous. The ABs are a bunch of old geezers like me. They gotta prove themselves, blood in blood out. Then the NLRs drove up and started competing with them. They'll kill each other to break rank. It's just a nightmare. But . . . [*Sighs.*] It's just protection. Because if you don't belong to them, then the Mexican Mafia or the Black Guerillas will kill you if they get one chance. If you're not picked up by the NLR or the AB, then you're dead. There's so many people that want to get in, and like [I] said earlier, you don't choose them—they choose you. You've got to be on your p's and q's, and once they choose you, you're going to do anything they tell ya.

How does the AB compare with other prison groups?

They're the most treacherous. The Mexican Mafia is pretty rough too. They're pretty tough. You're going to get stuck [stabbed] pretty quick if you cross them. It's a different life. But the AB, they sure can reach out and touch someone. Just like that commercial [for] the telephone service. They will reach out and touch you.

How do they do that?

Supposing I'm in the slam, right, and I got pissed off at somebody, and I want to kill you. I write a kite to one of my bros and I say, 'Dust this person.' Then, boom, you're dead. They pass messages through me—through people like me—through what we call kites. They're like messages, or visits.

What's your relationship with the AB now?

They have respect for me, and I have respect for them. Yeah, I'm a member of the Aryan Nations, the Aryan Brotherhood, but I have mellowed out. I'm old now, I'm 56 years old. I've done this all my life.

Survivors and Witnesses Speak Out

A Woman's Dark Skin
Provokes Hateful Reactions
After September 11, 2001

Chitra Divakaruni

Chitra Divakaruni is an Indian American novelist and poet. In the following narrative she reflects on the changes in national attitudes since the terrorist attacks of September 11, 2001. Before that time, she was accustomed to hearing inquisitive and respectful comments about her dark skin and about Indian food and culture. Since September 11, however, many people she encounters have reacted with anger to her non-Western clothing and her dark skin color, often mistaking her for an Arab. Even after these hateful experiences, she expresses her hope that people can acknowledge their differences but pay more attention to their similarities.

I confess: Vanity is one of my vices. Perhaps that's one reason I so enjoy living in the San Francisco area, where people are always walking up and telling me all the things they love about me.

"I love your outfit," says Elena, who works at the college where I teach. "It's so elegant! Is there a place where I can get one?"

I smooth down my salwar kameez with a not-so-modest grin and give her the name of a boutique in town.

"I love Indian food!" gushes a stranger on the train to Berkeley. "You're so lucky to be eating it all the time."

I briefly consider letting her know that I prefer Mexican or Chinese cuisine when I eat out. That in my home, where I live under the tyranny of my seven- and ten-year-old sons, pizza and French toast are far more common than raita and curry. But already she's asking if I know a good recipe for tandoori chicken. I dictate one of my mother's, which she takes down in her Palm Pilot, unaware that I'm drawing liberally upon my imagination to supply the spices that I've forgotten.

"I love your skin!" my friend Robin exclaims as we jog together. "Asian skin ages so well. Mine is just a mess."

I prescribe a regimen of a turmeric-paste mask once a week. Less sun. And a virtuous life. "Then perhaps you'll be reborn as an Indian."

"Yeah, right," she says, giving me a push, and we laugh as we cross Van Ness Avenue.

Reactions After September 11

But since the horrifying terrorist attacks, things have been different. People still look at me—but they aren't always admiring. I've seen people whispering to each other as they eye my salwar kameez, and I know that to some of them the loose pants and long tunic seem just like the clothes of the Palestinian women we all saw on TV rejoicing after the attacks. Well-meaning friends have e-mailed warnings that I should wear only Western attire, not go anywhere alone, and even buy a gun. I want to laugh off these suggestions, but I can't. Since the attacks, too many people have faced verbal or physical abuse, been ordered off airplanes, been beaten—or even been shot to death.

I've also been advised to display the American flag prominently on my house and car. This upsets me in a strange way. I love the flag, just as I love America and its commitment to liberty, equality, and justice. But it bothers me that my patriotism is suspect unless I put up a flag to demonstrate it. And why? Because I don't fit the public's notion of what a "good American" looks like.

The other day, as I was walking into the local grocery with my sons, a man shouted, "F***ing Ayrabs, why don't you go home!"

I hurried my children into the store, my face burning.

"Mommy," asked my younger son, "why was that man so angry? Was he talking to us?"

"What did he mean, 'go home'?" asked my older one. "We're from right here." I had no words with which to answer them.

Nothing Is Real Until It Happens to You

It is said that nothing is real until it happens to you. I'd read about the hate crimes that swept the country in the aftermath of September 11. I'd been upset and enraged—but when I saw this man, his face filled with hate for me and my children, something broke in me. My heart beating hard with fear, I became aware, as never before, that some people see a whole different side of otherness. The side that makes them say, "You aren't one of us. You don't belong here and you never will." The side that makes them say, "Go home."

Whether we like it or not, we now live in a fractured, global world in which the notion of home itself has become a complicated one. We move, living in new places but staying connected to the old ones where our parents and friends still live. In many cities, half the people we meet in the course of a day are nothing like us. Some of us embrace this difference with glad fascination; some push it away with angry insecurity. But in both cases, aren't we focusing on the wrong thing?

This is what I want to say to those who love my foreign looks and culture—and also to those who despise them. Be aware of my otherness, but don't give it so much importance that you lose sight of what lies beneath. Don't we all want the chance to be happy in the place we've chosen to call home? Aren't we afraid of the same things—hatred and violence, a war that might turn our fragile world into a wasteland?

In our hopes and fears, you and I are one.

Killed Because He Looked Arab

Joginder Kaur

After the terrorist attacks of September 11, 2001, some Americans reacted with fear and hatred toward anyone they believed might be Muslim. Arizona resident Frank Roque openly expressed his anger and told friends he was going to "shoot some towel-heads." On September 16, Roque drove by the Phoenix gas station owned by Balbir Singh Sodhi and his brother, Harjit. Sodhi was born in India. He was not a Muslim. He wore a turban because he practiced the Sikh religion. Sodhi was outside his gas station helping a landscaper plant flowers when Roque opened fire and shot and killed him. Roque later fired at a Lebanese clerk at another gas station and at the home of an Afghani family. He was caught by police the next day.

Sodhi's wife, Joginder Kaur, was living in India at the time. When Harjit called her to tell her what happened, she could not believe someone would hurt her gentle, loving husband. In the following selection, she writes about the pain and shock she experienced, but also about the warmth and kindness expressed by many Americans at her husband's funeral.

It was 3:30 a.m. on September 15 [2001] when my telephone rang. My brother-in-law, Harjit, was calling from Phoenix, where he ran a gas station with my husband, Balbir.

"I have terrible news," Harjit said. "You must come right away. Balbir has been shot."

Shot? How could that be? I thought. I had just spoken with him at 10 the night before. He had called me at home in Bassiwal, the small Indian village where I live with his parents. Balbir left for America in 1988 to join Harjit and his other

Joginder Kaur, "My Husband Was Killed Because He Looked Arab," January 2002, pp. 63–64. Reproduced by permission.

brothers, it was his goal to start a successful business and eventually send for me and our children. Two of our sons, ages 24 and 27, had already moved to America to be with him. I still live in India, on my in-laws' farm, with our third son. Our two grown daughters live near us, with their babies.

Last February, Balbir and Harjit opened a gas station in a newly developed section of Phoenix, where they also sold some groceries. There are not many stores in the area, so customers were glad to see it open.

Assurances from Far Away

On the night he was shot, we had a long phone conversation, one of many since the attacks on the World Trade center and Pentagon just four days earlier. Like everyone around the world, we had watched the news and were horrified. I told Balbir I was afraid for him and our sons. We had heard that foreigners were being beaten by some Americans who blamed the attacks on anyone who looked Muslim.

Our family practices the Sikh religion, a faith devoted to peace and prayer. My husband had dark skin and a beard and wore the turban that Sikh men wear (because Sikhs do not cut their hair). I was scared and told Balbir I wanted him to come home to India.

"Don't worry," he said in his kind, sweet voice. "We will be fine. We are far away from where the attacks occurred. The government will find who did this. We are safe." He then asked to speak to his father, who was already asleep for the evening.

"Tell him I'll call tomorrow morning at 11," he said. We said good-bye to each other, and I went to bed. Six hours later, Harjit was on the phone telling me my husband had just been shot to death.

"You're lying," I told him. I was angry, frightened. "Balbir is calling me at 11 tomorrow. You must be drunk."

I hung up on him, but he called back right away and spoke to my in-laws. He told them what he'd told me—that Balbir had been shot, and to come to Arizona right away. Eventually, he told them the terrible truth: Balbir had been murdered because of the color of his skin and his turban, because he looked like the terrorists. When it happened, he had been standing outside the gas station, looking at some flowers a landscaper had just planted. While Balbir and the landscaper were talking, a man drove by in a black pickup truck, aimed a gun out his window, and shot Balbir three times in the chest. One of my sisters-in-law, Surinder Kaur, saw the shooting from the store and rushed to Balbir's side. He died, almost immediately, in her arms.

Facing the Truth

Still, I refused to believe it. It was all too horrible. He was only 51. My in-laws were crying as they called family and neighbors to tell them what had happened. Within an hour or two, our house was crowded with almost 150 people. Many of them had family living in America, and they were very frightened. If Balbir could be killed, who would be next? I was in denial. I kept telling everyone, "Don't cry. Balbir is alive. He is going to call me at 11. He promised."

At 11, when the call didn't come, I still refused to believe the news that Balbir was dead. Finally, at 12:30 the phone rang. It was my eldest son, Sukhwinder, who lives in America. He began pleading with me, "Mommy, he is dead. You must believe this."

That's when the awful reality hit me. I started screaming and couldn't stop. Our family doctor was there, and he gave me sedatives to calm me down. I fell asleep immediately, and the doctor stayed by my side for a day and a half. When I awoke, I knew it was true: My husband was gone.

But a question nagged at me: How could anyone harm a man as gentle and loving as Balbir? He was the kindest man I had ever known. When I was 12, he married my older sister, and they had two children together. But my sister died giving birth to their third child. Family is so important to me, and I knew I could not let Balbir raise my sister's children alone. They needed a mother, and he needed a wife. Soon afterward, I married him, and our love for each other grew. I loved my sister's children as if they were my own, and today, they think of me as their mother. Shortly after our marriage, Balbir and I had two more children together. He was a good father and a wonderful husband. He called me everyday and told me how much he missed me. He worked hard to make sure our children had the best education. He was very proud that they all attended college.

He was also very proud of his business. It was clean, modern, and very pretty. Not many gas stations have flowers on their property, but Balbir thought they made his customers happy.

And customers did seem to love my husband. I could see this when I visited him last summer. Often, he gave free candy and sodas to local children. Harjit used to scold him for that, but he said, "The children look like small angels of God. Their hearts are pure and clean. They get one candy and they give us so much blessing."

Kindness of Many Americans

When my family and I arrived in America for Balbir's funeral, flowers and candles covered our gas station in tribute to him. Thousands of people came to a memorial service to honor his life. It was a heart-wrenching experience to bury my husband, but I drew comfort from the many people who came to celebrate his life. I was touched by the outpouring of support, but not surprised. Balbir and I had always been drawn to the kindness of Americans. And in the eyes of this nation, we were a family suffering and sharing a loss. I cannot blame all for the ignorance of one person.

Even though I am devastated, I have no hatred for my husband's killer. God put him on this earth, too. But I miss Balbir so terribly. I feel him all the time, in my heart, and I remember his smile and kindness. He had no enemies, nothing but love for people and his country. Tragically, he is just another innocent person lost to hate.

Frank Roque, the man who shot Balbir, has been charged with first-degree murder for Balbir's death and attempted murder for other subsequent race-related shootings. As Roque was led away by the police, he shouted, "I stand for America all the way!"

But he does not stand for the America Balbir loved.

Finding a Swastika in My Binder

Elizabeth Chase

Elizabeth Chase is a high school student and serves as an officer in both the campus Jewish club and the Jewish Student Union. In the following story, Chase describes the time when she found swastikas and anti-Semitic remarks scrawled in her student planner and more swastikas around her school. At first, she chose to forget about them. However, as she writes, the symbols provoked discussion among her classmates. When she overhears students talking about how Jews should put the Holocaust behind them, she is outraged. Chase decides then that is it important for her not to forget but to choose to remember and to stand up and talk about the hateful events of the past and of the present.

I am sitting in physiology class. The teacher assigns a lab report and I open my planner. I see something doodled on the page. I have a swastika in my planner. I turn the page, write down the assignment, and close the planner. And I forget about it until later that day.

I do not know who drew the swastika in my planner. I do not know why. I choose to believe that it was done by a bored kid, looking to vandalize someone else's forgotten things, that it is harmless. And I choose to forget about the swastika.

It is not until later that week I tell someone, a Jewish friend of mine. He wants to see it. I show him and he flips through the pages. He sees that there is more. Another swastika. Also written is "I love bagels," "zig heil" (meaning to salute Hitler) and "you suck." My friend is outraged, and he tells me I should turn it in to the office. It's a hate crime, he says. But I am not outraged. I don't know why. I try to forget. And I can't.

Elizabeth Chase, "The Swastika in My Binder," *Jewish Journal of Greater Los Angeles*, December 2, 2005. Reproduced by permission of the author.

Conflicting Opinions

My issue is not that it's written, but why. Who did it? Did they know? Know that I am Jewish? And if so, how? Because I am an officer of the campus Jewish club? Because I wear shirts from my Jewish camp? Because I have a Jewish star around my neck? Because I have Jewish holidays written in my planner? And I think to myself who cares why? Again, I choose to forget about it.

A few days later, I get into a discussion with two classmates. They think it is ridiculous that some Jews refuse to buy German-made automobiles. I tell them that my mom is one of those people. I say those companies profited from and contributed to the murder of millions. I also say that it's a choice that is private and up to each person. One of the girls says to me, "The Holocaust was more than 50 years ago. It didn't personally affect this generation. They should get over it and buy the cars." And now I am finally outraged.

Choosing to Remember

Yes, the Holocaust was 60 years ago. But it is not true that it doesn't affect individuals today. It forever changed the lives of families with murdered relatives and also those with survivors. For them, 60 years ago seems like yesterday.

I am lucky that my immediate family is free from the marks of the Holocaust, but my larger family is not. Six million people died in my family. And now, residual hatred of Jews has reached into my life. I have a swastika in my planner. And since then, two more swastikas were found on the restroom wall, and one carved into a tree.

I understand why I was outraged by the girl's comments. She told me and the entire Jewish people to forget. And I realized that that's what I had been doing. I chose to forget. I chose to ignore the hateful things directed at me. I chose. And now I know that hate is about choices. Choose to hate, choose to ignore hate, choose to deny hate, choose not to hate, choose to stand up in the face of hate.

So now I am choosing not to forget; I am choosing to remember. I remember by talking about this to my English class, and now they too are outraged. I remember by turning my planner in to the administration, so they can find and deal with the hateful vandal. I remember by taking notice of all of the hateful things I hear on campus and in my community. Before, I ignored these things. Now, I choose to acknowledge that hate exists. I choose to remember.

The Murder of My Transgendered Child

Sylvia Guerrero, interviewed by Patrick Letellier

In the following article Patrick Letellier interviews Sylvia Guerrero about the death of her transgendered child and about facing the killers during the trial. Guerrero's transgendered seventeen-year-old daughter, Gwen Araujo, was beaten and strangled to death by three men who discovered that Araujo was biologically male. In the interview Guerrero discusses her anxiety about the trial, about how Gwen's death impacted her family, and about discovering her child's sexuality. The first trial ended in a mistrial but the second trial brought two second-degree murder convictions against Araujo's killers. Patrick Letellier writes for many newspapers and magazines and is also an editor and teacher.

When 17-year-old transgendered youth Gwen Araujo was bludgeoned and strangled to death by three men who discovered she was biologically male at a party in October 2002, her death took a heavy toll on her mother, Sylvia Guerrero. A former legal assistant, Guerrero went on disability when her daughter's body was found in a shallow grave in the wilderness 150 miles from their Newark, Calif., home in the eastern San Francisco Bay area. And while she has been active in transgender activists' protests following her daughter's death, she is struggling to put her life back together. She has lost her job, was evicted from her home, and has had her disability payments come to a halt.

The trial of the three men charged with killing Gwen Araujo began on March 15 [2004]. Not long before, *The Advocate* talked to Guerrero about the trial and what she's learned about transgendered people.

Sylvia Guerrero, interviewed by Patrick Letellier, "A Mother's Pain and Defiance," *The Advocate*, March 30, 2004, p. 20. Reproduced by permission.

Advocate: *How do you feel about the trial?*

Guerrero: Nervous. And part of me is scared of the details. But I need to know. I'm that kind of mom. From the moment Gwen got to that party to her last breath, I want to know what happened.

I understand the past year has been difficult for you and your family.

They didn't just take Gwen that night—they took my whole life. The pain is still as intense as it was a year ago. Pearl [her oldest child] didn't work for a long time. Brandon [her 15-year-old son] now lives in Virginia with his father because he had a hard time handling this. He was in junior high when they discovered Gwen's body. One of the kids at school asked, "Is that your faggot brother they killed?" He used to get A's and B's, but his grades dropped to D's and F's.

What do you know about transgender issues that you didn't know before?

I didn't know what transgender meant. Gwen never used that word. But she knew who she was, and we were on the same page about that. We discussed the sex change she wanted, her name, all of it. But I never realized the suffering that goes with being transgendered.

A Mother's Intuition

When did you realize that Gwen was different from other children?

Before she was even 2. As a mother, you just know. She would always play with Pearl's Barbies, never with Tonka trucks.

How did she come out to you?

We were in our pajamas in my room, painting our toenails. She was 14. She said, "You know, I'm different. I don't feel like a boy." She said she felt like a freak, mad people always called her names. She said, "I'm not gay." I don't think at that age she knew what she was, but she knew she didn't identify with her body. I bought her clothes and makeup. I stood up for her. And I've been criticized for that, as if somehow I allowed this to happen.

What would you like other transgendered teenagers to know?

Never be ashamed of who you are. Hold your head up high and [strive] for the stars. Love yourselves for who you are.

How do you think the media have handled Gwen's death?

Not good. A lot of what they say is wrong. She was never buried in a dress, and her tombstone does not say "Gwen." Those murderers buried her—do you think she'd want to be buried now? No. She's in a wooden urn in my home. And it says, "Gwen Amber Rose Ara[u]jo." Amber Rose is the name I chose when I thought I was going to have a girl. On the urn there's a quote: "Fly free, our beautiful butterfly angel."

CHAPTER 3

Taking Action
Against Hate

From Hate to Hope

Keishuna Young

Keishuna Young was an eighteen-year-old African American high school senior when she was the victim of a racial attack. In the following article, she tells of when, on her way home from school, a white male began calling Young and her friend "niggers" and "losers" as he and friends passed by them in a car. The man returned a few minutes later and rammed her with his car. She was thrown from the hood of the car as it sped away and sustained injuries.

As a result of this incident, Young decided to form an organization which she calls Gwinnett Organized Teens, Hope of Tomorrow (GOT HOT) to promote peace, love, and unity among teens and to help promote positive change in the future.

My name is Keishuna Young. I am an 18-year-old senior. I am aspiring, one day, to be a high profile psychologist. I am also one of the most tolerable people until one defies my beliefs of civil respect toward all human beings. Here is my story.

Racial Slurs and Physical Attack

On January 16, 2001 something happened to me that I would have never thought to be possible. It all started when a friend and I were walking home from our bus stop. An unfamiliar car drove past us as the driver yelled out something that we couldn't quite understand. So we continued our conversation and our usual walk home. The unfamiliar car was crossing a speed bump and yelled out "NIGGERS". Knowing me, trying to avoid any type of trouble, we casually said they only yelled

Keishuna Young, "From Hate to Hope: A Young Teen Copes with Racism," *Blackgirl Magazine*, July–August 2004, p. 12. Copyright 2004 Blackgirl Magazine. Reproduced by permission.

"LOSERS". As we continued to walk we noticed the car dropping off some neighbors (might I add that I'd never seen any of these people in this car a day in my life). The driver turned his car around and yelled "NIGGERS" again. And again we did not respond. But the driver insisted that we respond so he yelled "NIGGERS" for a third time. By this time I was highly upset considering that this is the day after Dr. Martin Luther King Jr.'s birthday. This is also the day after I'd just written a statement about being thankful and appreciative for all of the people that went down in history fighting for our civil rights that opened up the doors for the opportunities that I have to this very day. (Note: For Dr. Martin Luther King Jr.'s birthday my family and I visited the King Center.) The whole time that this is happening to me I am in total disbelief and shock. I mean didn't I just write about how much I would love to see the world overlook racism, prejudice, and stereotypes so that we could live in racial harmony? I threw my things down and began yelling back at the driver. The next thing I know I am jumping straight into the air and landing on the hood of the unfamiliar car. The driver is still yelling and I am still yelling. The driver then swerves throwing me off of the car and onto the ground, where I received multiple wounds including one on my side that I must live with for the rest of my life. I jump up and continue yelling as the driver tries to speed away from the scene stopping at a speed bump yelling "NIGGER".

Living In Fear

I flee home banging on the door for my older sister to see me bleeding profusely. All I want to do is go to sleep and forget about the whole nightmare, but instead my friend, whom was with me at the time of the unpleasant incident, assists me with reporting to the police. My older sister takes me to the hospital where my mom meets me. I was so afraid and so disillusioned that I did not return to school for the following two weeks. I was afraid that he'd come back to finish me off with some friends or something. I was placed on different medications as well as treated by a surgeon, psychologist, and chiropractor. I could barely sleep after all of this went on. I couldn't turn back the hands of time so I decided to FOR-GIVE.

From Tragedy to Hope

It has always been a dream of mine to bring everyone together and just enjoy life. But before my whole incident it was just a sheer dream. But after this terrible "hate crime", my mother and I decided to turn this tragedy into a learning tool and to develop a program for teens to face this reality that still exist in Race Relations today. This is where the idea of GOT HOT comes from. GOT HOT is the acronym for Gwinnett Organized Teens, Hope of Tomorrow. Our mission is to promote peace, love, and unity throughout the world amongst the "next generation". Our youth is the future and we must make a change. GOT HOT has participated and developed several events to support our mission. These events include two of the most intriguing annual Unity Teen Dream Walks in our community that were held on Dr. Martin Luther King Jr. Day. To make these events successful we invited several different cultures to perform acts such as dancing, singing, and speaking about what Martin Luther King Jr. Day means to them. This event, successful both times, showed how easy it is to unite and have fun without discriminating and criticizing one another with racial stereotypes. Hopefully GOT HOT will transform into Growing Organized Teens, Hope of Tomorrow and continue the legacy of Dr. Martin Luther King Jr.'s dream. It is GOT HOT'S hope to have a Teen Television Show, which presents a diverse group of teens moving towards a more positive direction in Race Relations in America.

Fictionalized Accounts Can Be Reminders of the Reality of Hate Crimes

Daniel A. Olivas

On August 10, 1999, Buford Furrow, a self-described white separatist, walked into the North Valley Community Center near Los Angeles and began firing shots at those inside. Three children, a counselor, and a receptionist were wounded in the attack. Later that day Furrow shot and killed a Filipino postal worker before being apprehended by the police.

Daniel Olivas's 9-year-old son, Benjamin, was at the Community Center on the day of the shootings. Olivas and his wife did not know for several hours whether Benjamin had been hurt or killed. Olivas was prompted to write a short story based on this incident to remind people of the reality of hate crimes. In the following article, he talks about the day of the attack and his reasons for writing the story.

In late fall of 1999, I wrote a short story, "Summertime," which I eventually included in my collection, "Assumption and Other Stories" (Bilingual Press, 2003).

When the book reviews started coming in, most noted that particular story's unsettling premise. But what fascinated me more was the response I received via e-mail or in person from family, friends and strangers alike. More on that later.

"Summertime" begins benignly enough. The first section of the story has the heading, "6:53 a.m.," and we encounter a married couple having difficulty getting their young son ready for summer day camp. Claudio Ramírez and Lois Cohen obviously love their son, Jon, but as with most parents who must

Daniel A. Olivas, "First Person-Documenting Hate," *Jewish Journal of Greater Los Angeles*, August 12, 2005. Reproduced by permission of the author.

get to work, mornings can be a bit frustrating. Jon eventually gets dressed, fed and trundled off to Claudio's car for the ride to camp. The next section is titled, "7:39 a.m.," and we switch to a dusty, small hotel room where we meet a sleeping man named Clem whose "head looked like a pot roast as it lay nestled heavily on the over-bleached pillowcase." Clem wakes to begin his day. Clem is from Oregon and has driven to Southern California on a mission.

The story moves along, switching between the Ramírez-Cohen family and Clem. We eventually learn that Clem's "mission" is to perpetrate a hate crime. He eventually settles on the Jewish day camp that Jon attends. I paint Clem as an average person who feels belittled by the world and who hopes to have a "big day" that will put his face in every newspaper and on TV. He is no evil genius. But the evil he perpetrates is as harrowing and real as any better-planned hate crime.

The True Story

I wrote the story after we experienced the horror of Buford Furrow's attack at the North Valley Jewish Community Center (JCC), on Aug. 10, 1999. Furrow, a self-described white separatist, shot and wounded three children, a counselor and the receptionist at the JCC. That same day, he murdered a Philippines-born postal worker, Joseph Santos Ileto. Furrow admitted to wanting to kill Jews. He also stated that Ileto was "a good 'target of opportunity' to kill because he was 'non-white and worked for the federal government,'" according to then-U.S. Attorney Alejandro Mayorkas.

For almost four hours that hot, horrible day, my wife and I didn't know if our 9-year-old son, Benjamin, had been a victim. We huddled together with my mother-in-law outside the camp waiting for word. Unfortunately, because the police were concerned that the shooter or shooters were still in the vicinity, the children who had not been wounded had been whisked off to a safe house. A rumor ran through the crowd that a boy named Benjamin had been shot and killed. The agony ended only when, eventually, we were reunited with our son.

The Story Is a Reminder

Frankly, I'm having difficulty writing these words because the memories are coming back, full and clear. But that's one reason I wrote "Summertime." I wanted to use fiction to remind others that ordinary people living in today's world can be the target of hate crimes. And I also wanted readers to understand how easily hate-filled doctrines can be appropriated and acted upon by an "average" person.

Now back to the various responses to "Summertime." Most readers—particularly those who know my family—knew that Clem was based on Furrow. But several other readers had never heard of Furrow's attack on the JCC or his murder of Ileto. Those readers (most of whom do not live in California and who are not Jewish) expressed shock when I mentioned that the story was based on our own experience that day in August. And I expressed shock that they had not heard of the incident, particularly since it had received extensive (if not worldwide) news coverage. But this confirmed my conviction that writing about hate—even if fictionalized in a short story—can indeed educate the public about how easy it is for a person to become a Buford Furrow.

When I started writing fiction in 1998, I didn't feel that I had the moral authority to write about anti-Semitism. Though I had converted to Judaism 10 years earlier, my experience with bigotry was based on my ethnic identity as a Chicano. But after Aug. 12, 1999, I earned the right to talk about one particular act of hate against Jews. I will go further: I now have the duty to remind others of what Furrow did that day. Why? Because if we forget, we help create a climate where it could happen again and the Furrows of the world will have won. And I don't intend to be responsible for that.

A Hate-Crime Widow Forms an Organization to Stop Hate and Violence

Ginger Kolbaba

In July of 1999 a white supremacist named Benjamin Smith went on a shooting spree targeting Jews, Asian Americans, and African Americans. Ricky Byrdsong, an African American basketball coach, went for a walk with his children in their usually peaceful suburban neighborhood outside Chicago. Smith drove by and shot Byrdsong, who was rushed to the emergency room but died a few hours later.

In the following selection, Byrdsong's wife, Sherialyn, writes about the incident and about how her Christian faith led her to respond by forming the Ricky Byrdsong Foundation in order to help people recognize and overcome prejudice and hatred.

On July 2, 1999, my life changed dramatically. Early that evening, around seven o'clock, my husband, Ricky asked if I wanted to take a walk with him. I said yes, but first I'd promised my teenage sister, Jocelyn, that I'd give her a driving lesson. So Jocelyn and I took the car and left for the church parking lot down the street.

We were gone about 20 minutes. When we returned and were pulling into our driveway, I saw my eldest daughter, Sabrina, running down the street toward our house. She was crying, "Daddy's been shot!"

I couldn't believe my ears. I ran toward our house, but Sabrina said, "No, he's outside." So we ran up the street to where Ricky was lying. He was in terrible pain, writhing and moaning. A policewoman was already there. She told me, "He's been shot in the back, but there's not much blood. He'll be okay." I believed her.

I got on the ground and tried to reassure him. "Calm down, Ricky" I said. "You're going to be fine." Right before the ambulance arrived, the police asked me, "Do you know anybody who'd try to hurt your husband?" I couldn't think of anyone. Everybody loved Ricky.

Waiting

I called some friends to come and watch the kids. Shortly after I got to the hospital, my pastor and some friends joined me in the waiting area. I was concerned but I wasn't overly worried. I kept thinking, "He'll be okay. He'll be in recovery for a while, and then he'll be good as new." But an hour after we'd been waiting, a doctor told us Ricky had lost a lot of blood. The next report came an hour later. This time the doctor said the situation was grave. That was the first time I became afraid. I started to cry, then started to pray intensely for Ricky. Everyone was praying for him.

A little after midnight, the physicians came to the waiting room again. "We've done all we can do," one doctor said. "The bullet did a lot of internal damage. He lost a lot of blood." They told me they did their best to patch him up.

They allowed all of us to go into the critical care room where Ricky was. He looked swollen to twice his size. I stood over him and grabbed his hand. The group prayed for him, then I asked everybody in the room to leave.

I whispered in Ricky's ear that I loved him. Several weeks before, I'd memorized Ezekiel 37:9, which says, "This is what the Sovereign Lord says: 'Come from the four winds, O breath, and breathe into these slain, that they may live.'" I'd memorized that entire chapter, and I started to speak those words to Ricky: "Live! Live!"

Eventually a nurse came into the room. She stood there a long moment before saying, "He's dead, you know."

I looked at her in disbelief. "He's dead?"

"Yes," she said.

I started to sob, "No! No! No! No!"

Impact on the Children

Considering all that they've been through—all that they've lost—my kids have handled their dad's death extremely well. Losing a parent the way they did would have been a horrific experience for anyone—but especially for a child. I wish that Ricky Jr. and Kelley could have been spared the trauma of witnessing their dad's murder. But God has been faithful in comforting them and healing their emotional wounds.

Ricky Jr. experienced nightmares for a while, and when we went out in public, he'd look over his shoulder a lot. Now, whenever he hears a story about something tragic, he asks lots of questions. He wants to know every detail. I patiently walk him through all his questions.

I made sure that each of my kids went through intensive counseling. The counselor felt their faith and what they've seen modeled in other family and church members were having a powerful impact on them. I always try to remember that good will overcome evil. It's really about allowing my children the freedom to talk about it. I encourage them to discuss anything that's related to what happened to their father.

A Christian Response

Ricky was shot on Friday and by Sunday we knew that it was a racially motivated hate crime. My kids had seen the frequent news updates about Benjamin Smith's rampage through Chicago and the Midwest, shooting Jews and Asians and African Americans. So, we talked about it a lot.

I explained there's evil in this world, and the force behind that evil is Satan, and his spirit can incite people to kill. We talked about how some people have the wrong perspective about others who are of a different race or background. I explained that as Christians, that's not how we're supposed to live, and that most hate is rooted in fear and ignorance. But it's all really rooted in the spirit of evil.

I focused on Ecclesiastes 3, which says, "There is a time for everything . . . a time to be born and a time to die." I told them that we all have to die, and even though their father's death occurred at a young age, he'd lived a full life and had impacted many people. I tried to help them feel grateful they had a chance to know their father, and that he was able to instill things in them that they will always remember.

As for me, I faced a lot of anger. It was not so much that I was angry with Benjamin Smith as I felt anger against evil. In Ephesians 6:12, the apostle Paul says, "Our struggle is not against flesh and blood, but against the . . . powers of this dark world and against the spiritual forces of evil in the heavenly realms." That's where the real struggle is. Consequently I'm choosing to focus on breaking down the fear and ignorance that allow hate to grow.

People ask me if I feel robbed of justice because Smith killed himself. The answer is no. Our earthly years are temporal. For Christians, death isn't really the end; I'll see Ricky again in heaven. I also know that, someday every person will get his reward—good or bad. Benjamin Smith made his decision. Whether or not he took his own life, whether or not he'd been caught, whether or not he served a life sentence or got the death penalty in the end it's all going to be right and just. It's God who determines that. He is the just judge.

Building a Foundation

Today I'm pouring my energies into leading the Ricky Byrdsong Foundation, which seeks to arrest the growing epidemic of hate and violence among youth by building their character and instilling a sense of purpose. The reality is, no matter how much you educate or legislate, if you don't attend to matters of the heart and spirit, your problems will escalate.

So I'm working to help people recognize and overcome the kind of prejudice and hatred that led to Ricky's murder. When I speak to parents, I tell them to make sure they're not raising a person who defines himself by his hatred for others. As a parent, you need to be aware. What kind of music or magazines is your child listening to or reading? What's he doing on the computer? We must stay on top of what our kids are doing.

Also, we need to make sure we're not saying things that plant seeds of hatred. You may not even realize it. Suppose a parent says something such as, "It's not right for this school to admit a minority student with a lower grade point average rather than a white student." When you say those kinds of things, you may be putting thoughts in your children's minds such as, "Hey, they've taken away something I could have or my race could have."

The Ricky Byrdsong Foundation's primary focus is our youth program, Project Y.E.S.!—which stands for Youth, Education, and Service. We bring together youth from diverse ethnic backgrounds for our Corporate Camp, Not Just Basketball Camp, and Super Saturday Enrichment Days. In these settings, they discuss the stereotypes, beliefs, and issues relating to people different from themselves. They learn how to understand and appreciate each other's differences. Through their involvement in long-term, meaningful relationships, fear and ignorance can be greatly reduced.

Not having my husband here has been extremely difficult. I'm not going to pretend it's not. I've had to trust God when he says, "I am father to the fatherless," or that he'll be my provider, that he'll supply all my needs. I've had to trust God to keep his promises, and do the best I can.

From the time I was born to the day I said "I do," God knew Ricky's death would [b]e a part of my life. God orchestrated this platform I have. Therefore, I want to be faithful to my course, which is raising my three children, leading the

Ricky Byrdsong Foundation, and promoting racial reconciliation. I want to be true to the call God placed on my life, so that someday he will be able to say "Well done, good and faithful servant."

Hatred Brings Us Together

Richael Maile

In the following narrative, high school student Richael Maile, a white lesbian, and Ryan, an African American boy, encounter one another at a "wall demonstration" exhibit containing images of hate crimes. Maile writes that, although they had been contentious toward one another in the past, the exhibit helps the two realize how much they have in common.

Camped out in the quad at California's Riverside Community College in April 2003, those of us who belonged to the gay-straight alliance had just finished our "wall demonstration," depicting images of hate crimes inflicted on different groups of people. It followed the annual Day of Silence, during which students at schools across the nation express their support for gays and lesbians by taking a vow of silence.

I spotted my classmate Ryan heading toward me, and I armed myself for our usual debate. I've known Ryan for several years, and our relationship has been contentious. When I presented a high school project on same-sex marriage three years ago, Ryan and I had several heated discussions on morality. Ryan, an African-American who is now 16, is resistant to accept the validity of what he deems "unnatural" sexual orientations. Meanwhile, I'm a lesbian and an aspiring journalist and activist.

Ryan asked me about the images of Matthew Shepard [a gay young man who was beaten and killed in 1998], and I told him about what happened. "Richael, you're actually just like me," he responded, much to my surprise. Was this the Ryan I had pitted myself against for so long, repeatedly enduring his "Adam and Eve, not Adam and Steve" speech?

We stood there discussing the days of Jim Crow and the KKK. We realized that our perceptions of the world were similar, second-class citizenship, hate crimes, judgment of character based on outward appearance. That afternoon, bound by an unlikely adhesive, we found a plateau on which to stage our protest together. We are two people, separate in culture, who came together in a common struggle.

Turning Away from Hate

Elizabeth Moore

In the following article Elizabeth Moore describes her experience in a Canadian neo-Nazi organization called the Heritage Front. Moore writes about her introduction to the white supremacist movement, dealing with self-hatred, her experience writing for the movement, questioning the movement and eventually leaving the Heritage Front. The Heritage Front is a Canadian organization that seeks to promote the interests of white (Caucasian) Canadians and opposes immigration and multiculturalism. Elizabeth Moore now works to inform others about the dangers of groups like the Heritage Front and promotes antiracism education in Canada.

Neo-Nazis in Canada are often viewed as working-class, uneducated, under-privileged people—street-punks clearly on the fringe of society. This stereotype allows us to ignore them and to think "not in my backyard" or "not in my school." While it may be true that some of them are crazy punks, it is not true for all. I personally know, or know of, an estimated 17 neo-Nazis that are either students of, or alumnus of, eight post-secondary institutions in Ontario.

I can't explain why these educated people were attracted to the movement, for everyone has their own reasons. What I can do is tell you my story from the time I was first attracted to the time I left, and beyond, in hopes of explaining why and how it is possible for your friends, neighbours, or family to become racist extremists.

For a person to even be interested in joining a group like the Heritage Front they must have a certain level of pre-existing racism. And, admittedly, I was racist before I was introduced to the group. Many people think that racism is

Elizabeth Moore, Canadian Jewish Congress, 1997. Reproduced by permission.

mostly learned at home, and for many it is. However, both my parents are fairly liberal in this regard, so most of my racism was learned at school. I had white friends who complained bitterly about the "chinks" taking over our neighborhood. But, I also experienced the other side of the coin: I felt I was the victim of reverse racism. I was called names, pushed into lockers, and intimidated in my classes. At the time, I did not understand where my non-white classmates' rage was coming from, so their abuse only served to intensify the racism developing in me.

Being Introduced to the White Supremacist Movement

Five years ago, when I was in grade 12, I met a guy named Hans. Hans was different from other people I knew. He was German-born, for one, and a couple of years older than the rest of the class. I helped him with his assignments because he still had trouble with English grammar, and he, in turn, slowly introduced me to National Socialism. Eventually, he gave me a couple of flyers about the Heritage Front. He told me that they were "the white man's answer to muticulturalism." The flyers said they were a group of ordinary men and women concerned about the future of Canada, and persecuted by the Human Rights Commission for speaking out.

When I explain why I joined, I always feel torn because I want to believe I joined solely for political reasons: concern about the future, about immigration, about freedom of expression. But I realize now that that was only part of it. That was what was going on in my head. But what made me different from any other well-meaning, but ignorant, citizen, was what was going on in my heart.

Dealing with Self-Hatred

I had a lot of self-hatred, and resentment of not having control of my life either at home or at school. For a long time I internalized this negativity and felt that when I was unfairly criticized they were right. What the Heritage Front allowed me to do was to redirect the self hatred back out and thereby feel better about myself. What better boost to your self-esteem than to be told that you are a member of the most supreme race on the planet! Suddenly, what my non-white peers said to me didn't matter because they were "only blacks" or the fact that the Chinese were changing my neighborhood didn't matter because they would be deported when "we" took control. Finally, I began to feel more confident because I was not just sitting around and complaining. I was actually doing something, even if it was only reading propaganda material, and distributing flyers.

I was a willing recruit, but a slow recruit for them. For several months all I did was send away for magazines and talk on the phone with Wolfgang Droege [a founding leader of the Heritage Front]. Occasionally I sent money and distributed Heritage Front business cards.

However, that all changed when I wrote my first article for the Heritage Front's magazine *Up Front*. Ironically, my article was actually a criticism of a piece they published by David Lane. Lane, a member of the notorious racist/terrorist group The Order, is serving a life sentence in the USA for the murder of a Jewish radio personality. He wrote an article claiming that white women are corrupt and seduced by power. He claimed that the only way to "get the women back" was to reclaim them by force. I begged to differ. Not knowing that he was famous in racist circles, I assumed he was only a frustrated nineteen year old loser, and ripped his argument to shreds.

Becoming More Involved in the Movement

My article quickly became the most controversial one the Heritage Front ever published, and it also became the hook that Wolfgang and other Front members used to pull me deeper into the group. They worked on empowering me, by telling me that I was better than my family, friends and teachers because I was racially aware. They also congratulated me for standing up to Lane. They constantly told racist jokes and made racist remarks in order to saturate my conversations with racist rhetoric.

They introduced me to Holocaust denial literature, which came from 3 sources: Ernst Zundel [Holocaust denier and Nazi supporter], The Institute for Historical Review in America, and, other Front members. For example, Gerry Lincoln [a Heritage Front leader] gave me and my boyfriend access to videos in his extensive collection such as *The Eternal Jew* and *Triumph of the Will*. Holocaust denial is important to the movement because if a person is willing to believe that one of the worst mass human rights abuses in the history of the Western world was a hoax, dreamed up by the victims themselves, that person is willing to believe just about anything the movement's leaders tell them.

I quickly got hooked on the euphoria of hatred, the empowerment, and the sense of belonging, which I never had before. My attachment to the group grew so strong that I was always willing to do more, regardless of the potential costs, monetary or otherwise. By the time I was ready to leave the group, I was "staff reporter" for *Up Front*, I ran a telephone hateline, and I was a media spokesperson. I put up flyers, made speeches, attended demos, infiltrated left wing organizations, and public meetings, including one when Bernie Farber, the National Director of Community Relations for Canadian Jewish Congress [CJC], came to Queen's.

I basically lived the "Aryan Life," in which every action was seen as a contribution to the betterment of the race. This Aryan Life affected not only my political actions, but also my taste in music, clothing, TV and movies, to name a few. When I was ready to leave the group, my boyfriend, 90% of my friends, all my thoughts, my hopes and dreams for the future, were wrapped up in the Heritage Front.

A Film Stirs Doubts

The first time I had doubts was during the filming of *Hearts of Hate* in the summer of 1994. *Hearts of Hate: A Battle for Young Minds* was a documentary being filmed by independent film-maker Peter Raymont. The Heritage Front saw it as an ideal opportunity to get its message across—or so it thought. It was the first time I considered what others might make of my views, and so I answered the producer's questions carefully. At that time, I was also introduced to Eric Geringas, the associate producer of the film. He was, as far as I knew, a white guy in his late twenties. After my defection I found out that he was Jewish. As I watched this man work, I realized that he was actually a success. And I also realized that maybe, just maybe, the future for us young folk was not as bleak as the Front leadership led me to believe. I started thinking that perhaps, if I worked hard, there could be another future for me besides racist extremism.

In September of '94, when I returned to school I had a personal crisis in which I hurt people who were supposed to be close to me. I also experienced backlash from the film, since the *Hearts of Hate* crew filmed at Queen's University. I decided to lay low for a while, and fade out of my political life until I had the rest of my life under control. However, I found that to be impossible. I had telephone hateline commitments, and personal commitments to my boyfriend and other racist friends.

Seeing Through the Lies

By Thanksgiving of '94, everything started to unravel. Not only did I have personal dissatisfaction with my life, I also found out that I had been lied to by the Heritage Front leadership. I was finally told that the flyers that got Elisse Hategan charged for promoting hatred were actually Heritage Front material. Elisse defected from the Heritage Front about the time I became active. In order to get me in they told me that they had nothing to do with flyers she distributed that compared blacks to gorillas. The Front told me that they had even tried to dissuade her from distributing them! I realized that if they lied to me about that, there must be other things they were keeping from me. I began to see, with my own eyes, how much violence played a role in the group. And I also realized that they were not willing to treat women equally, and that I was an anomaly to them. Every other woman, except for Elisse Hategan, followed their boyfriends in and wanted to do nothing more than please them, and have many Aryan children.

With this new insight, I knew that I needed to do more than just try to fade out. I needed to defect completely in order to be free. I was afraid, and didn't know to whom to turn. Fortunately in November '94 Bernie Farber was invited back to Queen's to give a second talk about neo-Nazism in Canada. Through Eric Geringas, I got in touch with Mr. Farber. After his speech, which this time I didn't attend, we went out to a cafe, and had a long, very agonizing conversation. He told me I needed to stop doing the hateline, and break ties with all my Nazi friends, including my boyfriend. At the time, I didn't know if I could do it. He was asking me to give up life as I knew it. And honestly, I didn't know if I could trust him. I felt he had to have his own motives. After all, he was the enemy who was trying to put my friends behind bars.

Leaving the Heritage Front

After much soul searching, I decided to try and trust him. In December '94, when I was in Toronto for Christmas vacation, Mr. Farber invited me to his office for a chat. I had no idea what this so called chat would entail. When I arrived he asked me what my views were about the Holocaust. I was shocked! Every Nazi in Ontario would give an arm and a leg to be in the position to debate the Holocaust with the likes of Bernie Farber. But I couldn't do it. Somehow, sitting in his office in the CJC, my views, which I had promoted so fiercely, seemed unreasonable and unbelievable. So, I didn't respond to his question, I just gaped at him instead.

After what seemed like hours of him challenging my views, he invited me to the Holocaust Memorial Center in his building. The first thing he did was show me a wall of pictures of people who had perished in the Holocaust. He pointed out a picture of a woman with her smiling baby. It could have been taken anywhere, just like pictures anyone would have in their home. He said angrily, "That baby died in the gas chambers of Auschwitz, now you tell me what he had to do with any Jewish conspiracy." I couldn't respond, I couldn't even look at him. Next we sat and watched an audio-visual history of the Holocaust. As the images flashed across the screen, I realized that it was not the Jews, nor the non-whites, who were subhuman—it was me. And as I sat there beside Mr. Farber, I felt (I still can't find the right word for it) I felt "non-human". I felt like complete trash, and that I didn't deserve to live. After our meeting I said to him, you know, the Jews fought to keep their humanity when they had absolutely nothing, yet I had everything, and I freely gave mine away. Mr. Farber nodded his head and said, "Yes, but the beauty of humanity is that you can always get it back." As I left the building, I was actually able to smile to myself, because I knew that what he said was true, and that I would get mine back. What I didn't realize was just how hard that would be.

Five weeks after my meeting with Mr. Farber I had completely severed my ties with the Heritage Front. I was free in body but not in mind and still had a long way to go to recover myself. Suddenly, I was confronted with the fact that I had no identity. I had no idea who I was, where I was going, or what I wanted out of life. I also had to contend with the hatred that was still in me. This led to depression and even suicidal feelings. Many times I felt that everything was hopeless, that I could never fully recover, and that I would never again feel as strong and self-assured as I did when I was a

Nazi. I also had to face returning to Toronto for the summer with the realization that even though I had lived in that city for 19 of my 22 years, I did not have one friend left there. A year later that is still the case, and it is perhaps that feeling of being a stranger in my childhood home that upsets me the most about my situation.

Life After Hate

Despite all of the negatives, not everything since I defected has been bad. After the stress of final exams, and going public had subsided, I suddenly realized that I could do whatever I wanted. I could listen to whatever music, wear any clothes, watch any shows or movies I wanted, and decorate my place any way I pleased. I quickly took advantage of this new freedom. For the first time, I sat down and watched *Seinfeld* and enjoyed it immensely! I also took courses at Queen's such as 'The Holocaust of European Jewry 1933–45,' and I made a point of doing projects on Native Canadians, and black women civil rights activists in my other courses.

The most humbling experience since my trip through the Holocaust memorial, happened the following summer when I attended an international family reunion on my mother's side. My mother is of Mennonite descent, and many people at the reunion were Old Order, and wore traditional religious clothing. We all sat around and listened to stories about our ancestors who settled in Ontario, and one woman got up and explained that they came over from Switzerland, Germany, and Russia from the 16th century to the 19th century to escape religious persecution which included torture and murder, state sanctioned or otherwise. It was then I realized that hatred does not just affect the other guy, it can affect us, any of us, at any time for almost any reason. And it became clear to me that we are all equally human, and that if one person is a victim of hate, we all suffer for it.

CHAPTER 4

Hate Crimes
and Genocide

Witnessing My Father's Death in Turkey

Katherine Magarian

In the following article Katherine Magarian, an Armenian living in the United States, remembers her escape from the invading Turks during the time of the Armenian genocide from 1915 to 1917. Magarian writes of witnessing her father's death, her escape and subsequent separation from her mother, leaving the country, and eventually settling in the United States. The current Republic of Turkey rejects the idea that the events of 1915–1917 can be considered genocide despite the recognition by many countries that genocide did, in fact, occur.

I saw my father killed when I was 9 years old.

We lived in Palou [an Armenian enclave in Turkey], in the mountains. My father was a businessman. He'd go into the country selling pots and pans, butter, dairy products. The Turks, they ride in one day and get all the men together, bring them to a church. Every man came back out, hands tied behind them. Then they slaughter them, like sheep, with long knives.

They all die, 25 people in my family die. You can't walk, they kill you. You walk, they kill you. They did not care who they kill. My husband, who was a boy in my village but I did not know him then, he saw his mother's head cut off. The Turks, they see a pregnant woman, they cut the baby out of her and hold it up on their knife to show.

My mother and I, we run. They get one of my other sisters, and one of my other sisters, she was four, she ran away. My mother was hit by the Turks, she was bleeding as we go.

Katherine Magarian, "Voices of New England: Katherine Magarian," *Boston Globe*, April 19, 1998, p. B10. Reproduced by permission of the author.

We walk and walk, I say *Ma, wait, I want to look for my little sister,* but my mother slap me, say *No! Too dangerous, we keep walking.* It gets darker and darker, but we walk. Still, I don't know where. The Turks had taken over our city.

Two, three days we walk, little to eat. Finally, we find my sister, who had run away. Then we walk to Harput, and I see Turks and want to run, but they are friendly Turks, my mother tell me. She say, *You go live with them now, you'll be safe,* and I was. I worked there, waiting on them, cleaning, but I was alive and safe. But I don't see my mother for five years. She was taken to the mountains to live, and she saw hundreds of dead Armenians, hundreds of them, who had been killed by the Turks, bodies all over.

Years later, my mother say to the Turks, *I want to see my child,* and they let her come back. She came to the house at night. She did not know me, but I know it was her. Her voice was the same as I remember it. I tell her who I am, she say, *You are my daughter!* and we kiss, hug, and cry and cry.

Leaving the Violence in Turkey

My mother later heard of an orphanage in Beirut for Armenians, and we go there after the Turks kick us out of our country. I spend four years there, and again, I don't see my mother until a priest gets us together. In 1924, she comes to this country to meet family who left before the genocide. Three times now, I have lost my mother.

In 1926, I go to Cuba, with money from an uncle. On June 3, 1926, I marry John; we had met in Beirut and we marry in Cuba. He was a shoemaker and he came to the US in 1927, I came two weeks later, when I was 20. I had a baby in Cuba, alone, with relatives. That is my Mary. In all, we have four children, two boys, two girls, and also one other boy, but he died 40 days after he was born.

Life in the United States

We lived in Providence on Althea Street most of the time, 50 years. It was tough times in those days, but my husband he provided for us. He did not let me work, it wasn't the way. He say, *I bring one dollar home or I bring two dollar home, you no work, you stay home and take care of the kids.* I work very, very hard, but I do all for my children so they can be children.

It was a very nice neighborhood where we live. Italian people, Irish people, Armenian people, we all there, all the same. My kids, they only speak Armenian in the house and learn English in school. Education very important to us. We had no money to send the girls to college, but we save enough to send the younger boys, they go.

If I had been born later, here, I would like to be a nurse. My husband was sick for eight years, and I take care of him. He died at 88, in 1993. My mother and I were very close in this country, we saw each other a lot even though she lived in Pawtucket. In those days, it was much harder to get from one city to the next, but we still saw each other. She died in 1943. She was never sick, and one day she was gone.

I love to crochet and still do it a lot. I crochet angels for my nine great-grandchildren, so they all remember me, I give those to them.

Sometimes, near the anniversary of the slaughter, my mind goes back there. You know, when I was 14, maybe 15, I have a dream, Jesus comes to me, says *Give me your hand*, and I want to get up and go with him but I cannot get up. Then I am in the mountains, where all the dead were that my mother would later tell me about, and I see flowers, every kind of flowers, no bodies, it is beautiful. Then I see the ocean and a boat, the boat that would take me to Cuba years later. I think this was God saying to me that I would be OK.

I was lucky to live, I guess. God make me lucky.

My Family Was Massacred by Serbs

Hasan Nuhanovic, interviewed by Joe Rubin

In the following article Joe Rubin interviews Hasan Nuhanovic, a Bosnian writer whose family was massacred at Srebrenica by Serb army forces in July 1995. The Srebrenica massacre occurred as part of a war in the former Yugoslavia between Bosnian Serbs and Croats and Bosnian Muslims from 1992 through 1995 that eventually involved NATO forces. At Srebrenica nearly 8,000 men and boys were killed by Serb forces and buried in mass graves after being separated from their daughters, mothers, sisters, and wives. The corpses were later reinterred in secondary graves to cover up the crimes. Srebrenica had been declared a United Nations (UN) "safe area" under the protection of the international community at the time but was overtaken by Serb forces on July 11, 1995. In this interview Nuhanovic recounts his last moments with his family, the fate of his family, and the prospects for reconciliation in the region. Joe Rubin is a video journalist and has spent time in Sri Lanka and in Latin America as a Knight fellow, where he taught digital journalism in Panama, El Salvador and Ecuador.

Joe Rubin: Can you tell me about your experiences in Srebrenica?

Hasan Nuhanovic: I got stuck in Srebrenica with my family. That was not our original place. We used to live there a long time ago, and then we moved from one place to another in eastern Bosnia. Terrible things happened in eastern Bosnia. Between 1992 and 1995, we lived as refugees in that area without any outside assistance. We almost died of starvation with thousands of other people, and then in 1993, the United Na-

Hasan Nuhanovic, interviewed by Joe Rubin, "Srebrenica: A Survivor's Story; Interview with Hasan Nuhanovic," *WGBH*, 2006. Reproduced by permission.

tions sent the first peacekeeping unit of Canadians. There were only about 150 people there.

I went to their base to talk to them, and they hired me as an interpreter. Later, they were replaced by a Dutch batallion. There were about 600 Dutch soldiers, many more than the Canadians. They were supposed to protect us from the Serbs. The Serb troops were all over the place around Srebrenica. The area was about a couple of square kilometers. That was the only territory where we could live for three and a half years. We were, of course, prepared to accept that kind of life in misery, in total misery—no running water, no electricity, nothing. What happened in July 1995 was the final episode of genocide, of mass killing, of mass murder. The only thing I did not expect—because I expected bad things to happen— was that the U.N. [United Nations] peacekeepers, the Dutch battalion in this case, was going to assist the Serbs, to hand over these people to the Serbs, like my family. Later, thousands of mostly women and children, but also men and boys, moved toward the Dutch battalion. Some of them were allowed to come inside. But most of them were actually forced to remain outside the U.N. base. That was a decision of the Dutch battalion. They closed the gate. They sealed a hole in the fence. So about 5,000 or 6,000 people were inside the base, and about 20,000 people were outside the base. If you were inside the base, you were safe because the Serbs did not do anything bad to the people inside the base. I heard about killings happening outside the base. I heard screams and shots. I was afraid, of course, for my family, my parents and my brother—if they stepped outside the base, they were going to be killed. So I tried to keep them inside the base.

Everyone wanted to remain inside the base, but the Dutch decided to actually throw them out. They gave me a megaphone and said, "Tell the people to start leaving the base in groups of five." They didn't say anything else. The people didn't know what was waiting for them outside the base. They were hoping and thinking, "OK, the Dutch are in charge; the Dutch know what we're supposed to do, no problem."

Handed Over to the Serbs

Then what happened?

Some of the people, when they reached the gate, saw the Serb soldiers standing there next to the Dutch soldiers, pushing the men and the boys away from their sisters, wives, children—there was a separation taking place right there at the gate. People actually realized at that very moment that something is wrong, thinking, "I'm not going to any safe place. The Serbs are going to take me." The Dutch just stood there. Some of them turned around and walked back toward the factory [where the refugees were gathered inside the base] and forcibly expelled them.

And what about your family?

My family was among the last ones to stay inside. I tried to keep them inside the base for as long as possible. But they were forced. Three Dutch soldiers came inside with three U.N. military observers and looked at my family and told me, "Hasan, translate to your family, tell them to leave right now." I was crying. My brother, who was 19, was sitting on the chair. Of course, my parents knew what was going to happen. But they were behaving in a different way; they actually tried to calm me down—they felt that if I started panicking, I would cause trouble for myself. If their elder son, myself, could remain inside the base, could stay alive, let's at least try to do that. They knew my brother was going to be killed, they knew they were going to be killed. All the time as they were walked out of the base by the Dutch soldiers, my parents told me, "Hasan, stay. You can stay. Your brother will be with us; he will be OK." I was walking behind them, screaming and saying, "I am coming with you." But my brother turned around, and he started screaming right at my face: "You are not coming with me, you are going to stay inside because you can stay." And that was the last time I saw my family.

Did you ever learn what happened to your family?

I've heard so many stories. I've spent at least five, six years, every day, 24 hours, trying to find out what happened to them. I haven't the organization to do the exhumations; the identifications [agency] has not notified me of any findings. There is a DNA identification . . .

So they've never made. . .

Maybe they've been exhumed. Most of the remains are kept piled up in a facility. They are in very bad shape. Sometimes they only find a leg of a person or a skull. My cousin was killed, and his skull was found. I learned about it and I didn't know how to tell his father. How do you tell a father that your son's skull was discovered? I mean, it's a very difficult process. And I'm not really looking forward to that, to be frank. I don't know how I'm going to live through that.

Why General Mladic Was Not Arrested

Can you talk a little about your father and how he was asked to meet with General [Ratko] Mladic [a Serbian military leader accused of war crimes] at the fall of Srebrenica?

My father was a manager of a forestry company. He was a well-known man in the area; that's probably why people wanted him to represent them with the meeting with Mladic as one of the so-called negotiators. They were not negotiators, of course, because they were not in a position to negotiate.

There's a video where you can clearly see and hear Mladic talking to my father. My father tried to convey a message from 25,000 refugees that we are all civilians inside and outside the U.N. base, so please treat us as civilians. They were speaking on behalf of 25,000 refugees [driven out of the nearby town of Potocari]. There were three civilians, including my father, and Mladic apparently promised that everybody was going to be evacuated safely to the government-controlled territory.

When people talk about Srebrenica, they talk about three days in July 1995. But that's not Srebrenica. Srebrenica was three and a half years of life in a big concentration camp guarded by U.N. peacekeepers.

How do you feel about the fact that Mladic is still at large?

The question about why Ratko Mladic is still at large in my opinion has become a joke. It was a serious question in 1995, 1996, 1997. And now it's talking for the sake of talking. I used to sit down and read some reports and try to analyze why they were not arrested. But I'm not going to do it anymore because I'm just fed up. There was a capacity to do it, especially at the time when NATO had about 60,000 soldiers deployed in Bosnia, 20,000 of them Americans. There are only 6,000 soldiers now.

His Mother's Fate

Do you not think their arrest is needed for justice or for reconciliation? Would that change anything for you?

Yes. If you look at the big picture, their arrest is needed for the future, to actually settle the score, to have these two— The Hague Tribunal likes to call them the Two Big Fish—in The Hague, behind bars. But my point is that "the big fish" are important, but the small fish are even more important. One of the details about my mother's fate was that six Serbs in a nearby town in Srebrenica tried to rape her in prison. I got the story from a Serb who claimed to be there when it happened. She broke a glass on the window in the prison cell, and she cut her veins before they managed to open the cell door. Six Serbs. I know exactly the name of the chief of police who was in charge of the prison. And some other officials, police, the military civilian authorities, I know their names— they've not even been indicted or arrested or anything. Mladic and [Radovan] Karadzic [former Serbian politician accused of war crimes] are important for me as a citizen of Bosnia Herzegovina, for the Balkans region—for reconciliation. But for me personally, I would rather have first the information on who were those six soldiers who came to rape my mother when she killed herself. And what happened to this police chief?

I also learned that he [the police chief] is living in Sarajevo somewhere. Can you imagine? There's like a half million people in this town. I live here and this man is also living here, working in these so-called joint institutions that were created after the Dayton Peace Agreement was signed. What am I supposed to do if I meet him in the street? Am I supposed to go to him and say, "I'm Hasan Nuhanovic and you were chief of police 10 years ago in Vlasenica. What do you know about the death of my mother? What's going to happen?" This is a situation that should be resolved. And that's what I'm trying to point out.

Of course, Karadzic and Mladic are very important. But there is so much to be done even after they are arrested. Now there's this state court [in Sarajevo] with a war crimes chamber; I think as much as The Hague Tribunal was important, I think that the state court and war crimes chamber are maybe even more important. A whole process needs to unfold in the next five to 10 years in this country, in this capital.

Legal Action Against the Netherlands

Do you think Bosnia has been forgotten?

I think so. Bosnia seems to have been forgotten by the rest of the world. When something happens somewhere else, of course, you are worried that resources will be diverted. There should be enough resources left in this country to finalize the process they started. . . .

Did you get any recourse from the United Nations?

I did bring a case, and I am suing the Netherlands.

What are you hoping for?

Those who are responsible. The Netherlands protected those individuals. . . . I couldn't get to the individuals that wronged me because the state is protecting them. I am suing the state as an individual ... perhaps compensation.

The Failure of NATO and the UN

Tell me a little bit about the book you have written.

The title of my book is *Under the U.N. Flag: The International Community and Genocide in Srebrenica*. Actually, the massacre was happening while the U.N. flag in Potocari, the U.N. base, was still on top of the headquarters building. The massacre committed in Srebrenica against my people was done by the Bosnian-Serb army and police. But the role of the international community—the U.N. peacekeepers, the United Nations in New York, the European Union and NATO [North Atlantic Treaty Organisation]—were very, very shameful because many things could have been done to prevent the massacre. And these many people—the 10,000 who were killed—could be alive today if the United Nations, the E.U. [European Union] negotiators and NATO—with its airplanes in Italy at the disposal of the United Nations in Bosnia—all they needed was a call to take off from Italy and bomb the Bosnian-Serb troops on the ground on that very day. My book explains why this did not take place—why military intervention with very limited objectives did not happen. We did not need NATO to bomb the entire Serb army, but to bomb several of the Serb tanks on the ground. Destroy the tanks, and the Serb infantry would have stopped its attack. And the massacre would not have happened.

I'm trying to raise many questions in my book, and I'm trying to answer all the questions as well. And I quote from many documents. I'm talking about the U.N. documents labeled "strictly confidential"; most of those documents I got from an American reporter, David Rode, who wrote a book on Srebrenica called *End Game*. He's a friend of mine; he's done also good research on Srebrenica. Today, 10 years later, you can clearly see that the Dutch on the ground, in my opinion, are complicit in this war crime. And the role of the United Nations—and not calling for air strikes when air strikes were needed and when NATO planes were available—is also complicit. The United Nations should answer for this. At one point [documents say], the United Nations called off air strikes just as they started. Two bombs were dropped; they missed their targets and it was called off. Most documents say it was done by a Dutch minister of defense—a Dutch secretary of defense—and the United Nations basically complied with his request.

A Deal Between the UN and Serbia?

You uncovered in your book and in your research that there were actual deals made that allowed the massacre to happen.

Yes, there are various sources of information suggesting that a deal was made a month before the attack on Srebrenica when General Mladic was apparently promised by the top U.N. officials—a French general was involved and probably a British general and some more officials from the Western governments—that they would not bomb his troops on the ground anymore; they would send no more air strikes against his forces. So, again, according to this source, Mladic then knew a month before that if he attacks the eastern enclaves, one of which was Srebrenica, there will be no retaliation against his forces on the ground by NATO. At the very last moment, however, according to what I saw from being there, and from these documents, they did send two Dutch jet fighters, which dropped two bombs, which missed their targets, maybe deliberately; I don't know. And according to one source, these two bombs were actually from the Second World War.

It's easy to criticize all the things that the international community has done wrong, but there was a huge war going on and there was genocide going on here and they did do something.

I mean, come on. The only thing the U.N. peacekeeping troops in Bosnia did during the war was secure the route for human aid convoys. So basically, you feed the people before they get killed. That's exactly what happened in Srebrenica until Americans got involved directly. That's a fact. And I think we should appreciate that.

Witnessing Genocide in Rwanda

Uwera

In the following article Uwera describes her experience dealing with the genocide in Rwanda as a young girl. Uwera writes about her introduction to ethnic hatred in school, the death of her parents, her escape from a massacre, and the hope for justice in Rwanda. The genocide in Rwanda resulted in the deaths of an estimated 500,000 ethnic Tutsis and thousands of moderate Hutus. The killings were primarily carried out by two extremist Hutu militia groups—the Interahamwe and the Impuza-mugambi—over a three-month span in 1994. The response of the United Nations was slow and inadequate and countries such as the United States, France, and Belgium did little to stop the Rwandan genocide. The killing subsided when the Rwandan Patriotic Front, a Tutsi-dominated rebel movement led by Paul Kagame, overthrew the Hutu government and seized power.

There were 9 children in our family—5 girls and 4 boys, plus my father and mother. Our parents were farmers and cattle breeders. We lived off the land from harvests, milk and dairy products. I was the eldest and I loved my brothers.

It wasn't easy at school—my school friends, Hutus and those with whom I walked to school said that I was a Tutsi. What helped me was that there were lots of us. Our teachers would say to us, "Tutsis, stand up!" we would stand up and the Hutus stood to one side. We never studied with the Twa's and our teachers would write down the number of Hutus and Tutsis. There were those who didn't dare stand up but they were made to by force. That's why everyone at school knew the ethnic origins of their friends.

Uwera, "Testimonies from the Children," *Hearing and Healing: A Remembrance Initiative for Rwanda*. Reproduced by permission.

At home we were all Christians of the Catholic faith. We used to go to Mass.

At home lots of things were destroyed to such an extent that nothing from before the war can be found. I only remember our choir. If someone was getting married, we would sing and dance for them.

"Our Neighbours Began to Hate Us"

When I was in the 5th year (aged 12–13), I discovered I was a Tutsi. School friends taunted me saying we were Tutsis, hypocrites, snakes, etc. I didn't pay too much attention to that but later on I realised that it was a serious problem.

In 1990 when the FPR [Rwanda Patriotic Front] attacked the country, our neighbours began to hate us; after the death of [Fred Gisa] Rwigema [founding member of the FPR], we went to school. In the morning we would go and salute the national flag, but in the meantime we had been taught a military chant which implicated the inyenzi inkotanyi. We would sing it when we were in a procession. And so we took the trunk of a banana tree and we hugged it, saying it was the body of Rwigema. The person in charge of our school, called young Tutsis and ordered them to carry the body referred to and bury it. There was a young boy who was made to recite a poem insulting Rwigema at the spot where people had gone to bury him.

All along the path, the Tutsi boys who carried the body of Rwigema were surrounded by young Hutus who were saying: "The Tutsis planned the massacre of the Hutus and it hasn't worked: in our turn we will show them who we are."

We no longer have a good relationship with our neighbours. One good morning, my little sister went to get water from their well and they sent her away, saying that my father knew something about the arrival of the FPR—inkotanyi and their programme.

When they started arresting the Ibyitsos [accomplices] my uncle was the first to be pursued. He was a teacher at the primary school. He was imprisoned in 1990, but came out in 1991. At the time of threats and taunts, the Tutsi families didn't know how to defend themselves. They were expecting death any day. We had no right to complain.

I didn't know much about political parties, and I wasn't a member of one. I only heard about meetings of the MRND [National Revolutionary Movement for Development] which wanted to take over members of other political groups.

The Start of the Genocide

When the genocide was about to start, I told myself that the Hutus knew what was about to happen. For example in our village you could see Hutus with new machetes. They had big stones and lots of them would come to sharpen their machetes. There really were a lot of them. I can even show you the very place today. I told myself no-one could possibly kill his own cousin with a machete. And yet some of them said, when they were drunk, which ones they would kill before others. One of them said: "I will kill. . . ." It was my father's name they mentioned. The reason was that my father had refused to give him cow dung. From then on, he bore him a grudge, only I don't know whether it was he who killed my father.

We heard about the death of Kinani on the morning of 7th April on Radio Rwanda. I had just spent two days at my grandmother's. The day I was due to return home, they announced on the radio that nobody could leave their homes. Since I didn't know what to do, I stayed there. On the morning of 8th April, there were Hutus who worked the land at my grandmother's who came from the neighbouring district. She begged them to accompany me. Two men came with me as far as the house, then left.

At the house we were afraid, but we weren't always there. We had the idea of escaping when we saw Tutsis who had escaped the massacres in another district passing close to our home. Some of them had suffered from arrow attacks and still had the arrows stuck in their bodies. My father told us we had nowhere to go because even those who were at the church were expecting the murderers. Also it wasn't easy to cross the border into Tanzania. We were told that those who tried to flee by that route were thrown by the Hutus into the River Akagera. The Hutus had been patrolling the border for several days so that the Tutsis could not escape. We didn't know where to go or what to do.

Witnessing a Massacre

The massacres started on the 15th. Our father asked us to go and hide. I was with my little sister and we went to hide in a WC [water closet] in the bush. We spent the night there. An old lady lived in the vicinity in a hut; this is where my mother and her baby were hiding. She had only given birth the week before. In the morning my other little sisters, also went to hide at the old lady's but they were bleeding a lot—one had been hit on the neck with a machete and the other had been hit on the head with clubs. Where I hid with my little sister, Solange, necrophages had climbed on her body and I was busy removing them. From where I was hiding I could see all the murderers who were going to the old lady's where my mother and her baby were hiding. And so I saw people I knew amongst the killers. They said to the lady: "If you are hiding Tutsis, it will cost you dear." Then they asked her to leave quickly. Suddenly they burned the house. My mother ran out with the baby on her back and was hit on the head with a hammer. She died there and then. The house continued to burn and my two little sisters who were bleeding a lot could not get out. They burned to death inside.

I stayed In the WC with my little sister and had to wait for nightfall to go and see the baby. He was still crying. I went out at around 6pm. My mother was bleeding from her ears and nose I didn't have the strength to take the baby who was still on my mother's back, and I wasn't able to breast feed him anyway. So my little sister and I left them behind. A few metres further on, we met some other people who had hidden and we made our way together.

To Tanzania and Back

At this time, I had no news of my father and brothers. When I was hiding in the WC, I didn't move about or eat. Also throughout the genocide and even afterwards, I had secondary amenorrhoea. A year later everything returned to normal. Later on, we took the road and I left my little sister at my grandmother's. When I arrived at the house of a Tutsi who had the identity for becoming a Hutu was afraid of welcoming us, but after a while he asked us to go and hide in the reeds and to go back to his house at nightfall. We had left the town when the group of militiamen passed by. There was also a handicapped Tutsi. Since the killers didn't believe one man's identity, they tested him out by giving him the machete to kill the handicapped person. He couldn't do it so they killed him straight away and then killed the handicapped man. That evening we went back to that man's house and found him dead. So was the handicapped man. We didn't stay there long and afterwards went towards the southern districts. We were dispersed by the group of *interahamwe* militiamen whom we met along the way. This time we hid in the sorghum plantations and the killers sent dogs to hunt for us. This group of killers included people who looked after our cows. When they discovered me they said: "Don't be frightened. We don't kill women or girls. On the other hand we are looking for Hutu husbands for Tutsi girls because there are no more Tutsi boys alive." I was led to Tanzania to the Banako refugee camps. I was one man's wife. A week later, a family who used to live next to us, advised me to leave him and to return to Rwanda. It was a difficult thing for me to do, but I managed. I came back to Rwanda and the man stayed in Tanzania. A short while afterwards he died there from dysentery. Before returning I slept with him. Today I have no symptoms and I haven't had any investigative tests. I'm frightened but I show no signs of illness.

We went to see the ruins of our home and after destroying this camp we came back home through the remains. We occupied the house of a Hutu who was still in Tanzania. I lived there with the rest of another person's family. During this time, I didn't want to live in Rwanda because of everything I could see. I wanted to be alone, I didn't walk to talk to anyone. I think the reason for that was that I had no surviving brothers or sisters. I try to carry on living because I can see that I am not the only person suffering.

Current Life

I am afraid especially at night. I see people wanting to kill me with machetes and axes, and I start screaming. I am currently living with my maternal aunt and I have just finished secondary school. My aunt is trying to solve my problems from day to day. She loves me so much and I help her with everything.

When I see a Hutu, killer or otherwise, I feel bad and hate him. I no longer want to see him and he really makes me feel uneasy!

The reason why I was slow returning to school was because I didn't feel capable of doing so. I didn't think my brain was functioning normally. I couldn't see the importance of studying and I preferred to stay at home.

Justice and Genocide

When I saw the *interahamwe* coming out of prison, I was frightened and lost my nerve. I no longer want to comment on the Gacaca [a court system established in 2001 in Rwanda to deal with charges of genocide and war crimes] legal decisions. We witnessed the terrible things done by the killers and they have been released from prison!

Gacaca can never bring our loved ones back to life. Those who want to go there, let them go! I never will! Another thing about Gacaca is that the detained families won't tell the truth. For example, when they are asked where their neighbours have gone, or the families in such and such area, they do not reply. You can't find anyone who dares to tell the truth, admitting responsibility for the killings, and I wonder where they are? Are they in heaven? How did it happen?

As for me, I can't forgive any genocide killer for their wickedness. They knowingly did so much evil. They free those who are in prison and that is fair!!! They insult us day and night saying: "What good have you done imprisoning the Hutus?" as if it was really us who asked them to harm us!

I know one important man who handed out the machetes. He gave them to the Hutus so that they could work together.

Lessons Learned from the Genocide

What I have learned from the genocide is to find out who your real friends are, and who your enemy is. We have also discovered how to behave in front of others and those who welcomed us into their families, taking so many risks. One other thing is how to solve my problems myself.

Organizations to Contact

The editors have compiled the following list of organizations concerned with the issues debated in this book. The descriptions are derived from materials provided by the organizations. All have publications or information available for interested readers. The list was compiled on the date of publication of the present volume; the information provided here may change. Be aware that many organizations take several weeks or longer to respond to inquiries, so allow as much time as possible.

American-Arab Anti-Discrimination Committee (ADC)
4201 Connecticut Ave., Washington, DC   20008
(202) 244-2990 • (202) 244-3196
e-mail: adc@adc.org
Web site: www.adc.org

The American-Arab Anti-Discrimination Committee (ADC) is a civil rights organization committed to defending the rights of people of Arab descent and promoting their rich cultural heritage. It is active in the political arena as well as providing legal advice and referrals. The Web site includes a section on education which gives facts and lesson plans about Arab Americans in general and about discrimination in particular.

American Civil Liberties Union (ACLU)
125 Broad St., 18th Floor, New York, NY   10004
(212) 549-2585
e-mail: aclu@aclu.org
Web site: www.aclu.org

The American Civil Liberties Union works to preserve the civil rights of all Americans and to extend rights to segments of the population that have traditionally been denied their rights. Issues explored on the Web site include immigrants' rights, lesbian and gay rights, racial justice, and religious liberty.

Anti-Defamation League (ADL)
823 United Nations Plaza, New York, NY   10017
(212) 490-2525
Web site: www.adl.org

The Anti-Defamation League is a human relations organization that fights anti-Semitism and all forms of prejudice and bigotry. "Combating Hate" is the title of one section of the organization's Web site. Publications include the book *Hate Hurts: How Children Learn and Unlearn Prejudice*, and *101 Ways to Combat Prejudice*, a printable pamphlet available on the Web site.

Aryan Nations
PO Box 719, Lexington, SC   29071
(803) 233-6601
e-mail: NationalDirector@aryan-nations.org
Web site: www.aryan-nations.org

The original Aryan Nations group is an antigovernment, anti-Semitic group composed of people of white (non-Jewish) European descent which was founded in 1974 by Richard G. Butler. This is one of several sub-groups formed from the original Aryan Nations group. The group fights to safeguard the existence and reproduction of the Aryan race and the purity of Aryan blood. General information can be found on the Web site's "about us" page. Printable leaflets are also available on the Web site.

Aryan Nations: Church of Jesus Christ Christian
PO Box 151, Lincoln, AL   35096
(205) 616-6497
e-mail: conquerwemust@gmail.com
www.twelvearyannations.com

The original Aryan Nations group is an antigovernment, anti-Semitic group composed of people of white (non-Jewish) European descent which was founded in 1974 by Richard G. Butler. This is one of several sub-groups formed from the original Aryan Nations group. The group's purpose is to preserve the white Aryan race and to establish a separate Aryan state, which they believe to be ordained by God. In addition to what is available on the Web site, the organization will send information by mail for a small donation.

Center for Democratic Renewal
PO Box 50469, Atlanta, GA   30302
(404) 221-0025 • fax: (404) 221-0045
e-mail: info@thecdr.org
Web site: www.thecdr.org

Founded in 1979 as the Anti-Klan Network, the Center for Democratic Renewal is a multiracial organization that advances the vision of a democratic, diverse, and just society, free of racism and bigotry. It helps communities combat groups, movements, and government practices that promote hatred and bigotry and is committed to public policies based on equity and justice. Publications include *Near the Cross: A Ten-Year Chronology* and *Epidemic of the Hangman's Noose in the Workplace.*

Center for the Study of Hate and Extremism
Department of Criminal Justice, San Bernardino, CA   92407
(909) 537-7711
e-mail: blevin8@aol.com
Web site: hatemonitor.csusb.edu

The Center for the Study of Hate and Extremism at California State University, San Bernardino, is a nonpartisan domestic research and policy center that examines the ways that bigotry, advocacy of extreme methods, or the use of terrorism deny civil or human rights to people on the basis of race, ethnicity, religion, gender, sexual orientation, disability, or other relevant characteristics. The Web site provides research reports, current news, and a picture gallery of graphics that are used to promote hate.

Human Rights Campaign (HRC)
1640 Rhode Island Ave. NW, Washington, DC   20036
(202) 628-4160 • fax: (202) 347-5323
e-mail: hrc@hrc.org
Web site: www.hrc.org

The Human Rights Campaign works to achieve equal rights for lesbians, gays, bisexuals, and transgender persons. "Hate crimes" is included in the "Issues" section of the Web site. *A Chronology of Hate Crimes* and *A Decade of Violence* are available as online publications.

Leadership Conference on Civil Rights
1629 K St. NW, 10th Floor, Washington, DC   20006
(202) 466-3311
Web site: www.civilrights.org

Leadership Conference on Civil Rights is a coalition of over 190 national human rights organizations. Its mission is to promote the enactment and enforcement of effective civil rights legislation and policy. The Web site's section on hate crimes covers current information on hate crimes legislation and includes various fact sheets and reports.

National Alliance
PO Box 90, Hillsboro, WV   24946
(304) 653-4600
e-mail: national@natvan.com
Web site: www.natvan.com

National Alliance is a white nationalist organization made up of people of white, non-Jewish European ancestry. The group seeks to create a "homeland" area for a white Aryan society that excludes any Semitic and African influence or culture. Basic information on the organization, printable leaflets, and transcripts of a radio show called *American Dissident Voices* are all available online. There is also an online catalog of books and videos approved by the National Alliance.

National Association for the Advancement of Colored People (NAACP)

4805 Mt. Hope Dr., Baltimore, MD   21215-3297
(410) 580-5777 • fax: (410) 486-9255
Web site: www.naacp.org

The mission of the National Association for the Advancement of Colored People is to ensure the political, educational, social, and economic equality of rights of all persons and to eliminate racial hatred and racial discrimination. The organization lobbies in favor of civil rights legislation at the national level and also assists local branches with lobbying efforts. The NAACP publishes *Crisis Magazine*, which can be found online at www.thecrisismagazine.com.

National Gay and Lesbian Task Force (NGLTF)

1325 Massachusetts Ave. NW, Suite 600
Washington, DC   20005
(202) 393-5117 • fax: (202) 393-2241
e-mail: thetaskforce@thetaskforce.org
Web site: www.thetaskforce.org

The National Gay and Lesbian Task Force is a national civil rights advocacy organization for the gay, lesbian, bisexual, and transgender (LBGT) community. It provides local and national training and lobbying on LBGT issues. Research reports, facts, and statistics are provided on the Web site.

People for the American Way Foundation

2000 M St. NW., Suite 400, Washington, DC   20036
(202) 467-4999
e-mail: pfaw@pfaw.org
Web site: www.pfaw.org

The People for the American Way Foundation supports respect for individual liberty, celebration of diversity, love of country, and of the democratic institutions at its core. Hate crimes legislation is one of many causes which it supports. Current information can be found on the Web site.

Southern Poverty Law Center (SPLC)
400 Washington Ave., Montgomery, AL   36104
(334) 956-8200 • fax: (334) 956-8488
Web sites: www.splcenter.org

Tolerance.org, the Web site of the Southern Poverty Law Center, is an online source of resources for people interested in dismantling bigotry and hatred and replacing them with communities that value diversity. The Web site includes separate sections for kids, teens, parents, and teachers. Publications are available online or print copies can be ordered. Some titles are: *10 Ways to Fight Hate, 101 Tools for Tolerance*, and *Respond to Hate at School.*

White Aryan Resistance (WAR)
PO Box 2267, Temecula, CA   92593
(615) 676-4109
e-mail: warmetzger@aol.com
Web site: www.resist.com

The White Aryan Resistance is a white nationalist organization founded by former Ku Klux Klan leader Tom Metzger. Positions of the organization on over a dozen topics can be found on the Web site, along with an online newsletter and streaming audio of *Insurgent Radio* programs.

For Further Research

Books

Ricardo C. Ainslie, *Long Dark Road: Bill King and Murder in Jasper, Texas.* Austin: University of Texas Press, 2004.

Tom Alibrandi with Bill Wassmuth, *Hate Is My Neighbor.* Moscow: University of Idaho Press, 1999.

Donald Altschiller, *Hate Crimes: A Reference Handbook.* Denver: ABC-CLIO, 2005.

Robert M. Baird and Stuart E. Rosenbaum, eds., *Hatred, Bigotry, and Prejudice: Definitions, Causes & Solutions.* Amherst, NY: Prometheus, 1999.

Raphael S. Ezekiel, *The Racist Mind.* New York: Viking, 1995.

Phyllis B. Gerstenfeld and Diana R. Grant, eds., *Crimes of Hate: Selected Readings.* Thousand Oaks, CA: Sage, 2004.

Phyllis B. Gerstenfeld and Diana R. Grant, eds., *Hate Crimes: Causes, Controls, and Controversies.* Thousand Oaks, CA: Sage, 2004.

Gregory M. Herek and Kevin T. Berrill, *Hate Crimes: Confronting Violence Against Lesbians and Gay Men.* Newbury Park, CA: Sage, 1992.

Elinor Langer, *A Hundred Little Hitlers: The Death of Mulugeta Seraw and the Rise of the American Neo-Nazi Movement.* New York: Metropolitan, 2003.

Jack Levin and Gordana Rabrenovic, *Why We Hate.* Amherst, NY: Prometheus, 2004.

John W. Phillips, *Sign of the Cross: The Prosecutor's True Story of a Landmark Trial Against the Klan.* Louisville, KY: Westminster John Knox, 2000.

Tamara L. Roleff, ed., *Current Controversies: Hate Crimes.* San Diego, CA: Greenhaven, 2001.

Caryl Stern-LaRosa and Ellen Hofheimer Bettmann, *The Anti-Defamation League's Hate Hurts: How Children Learn and Unlearn Prejudice.* New York: Scholastic, 2000.

Mamie Till-Mobley and Christopher Benson, *Death of Innocence: The Story of the Hate Crime That Changed America.* New York: Random House, 2003.

Mary E. Williams, ed., *Opposing Viewpoints: Hate Groups.* Farmington Hills, MI: Greenhaven, 2004.

Periodicals

Keith A. Beauchamp, "The Murder of Emmett Louis Till: The Spark That Started the Civil Rights Movement," *Black Collegian*, February 2005.

Kirsten Betsworth and Molly M. Ginty, "Legacy of Hate: After Seven Long Years, I Finally Left My Husband and His Racist White Pride Group. Now All I Have to Do Is Save My Children," *Good Housekeeping*, July 2001.

Rachel Breitman, "Fighting Bullying, Especially Gay-Bashing, in Schools," *New York Amsterdam News*, June 16, 2005.

Margena A. Christian, "Emmett Till's Legacy 50 Years Later," *Jet*, September 19, 2005.

Pamela Colloff, "Jasper: What Happens to a Town Identified with One of the Worst Hate Crimes in American History?" *Texas Monthly*, December 2003.

Journal of Blacks in Higher Education, "Lies, Damned Lies, and White Supremacist Statistics," Spring 2000.

Brad Knickerbocker, "National Acrimony and a Rise in Hate Crimes," *Christian Science Monitor*, June 3, 2005.

John Leo, "Pushing the Bias Button," *U.S. News & World Report*, June 9, 2003.

Patrick Letellier, "A Mother's Pain and Defiance," *Advocate*, March 30, 2004.

Daniel Mandel, "Crying Wolf," *National Review*, March 13, 2006.

Rebecca McClanahan, "Klan of the Grandmother," *Southern Review*, spring 1996.

Pat McGann, "Coming to Terms with White Responsibility for Racist Violence: My People?" *Voice Male*, summer 2002.

Bob Moser, "The Murder of a Boy Named GWEN," *Rolling Stone*, February 24, 2005.

Edward Rothstein, "Hate Crimes: What Is Gained When Forbidden Acts Become Forbidden Beliefs?" *New York Times*, September 19, 2005.

Richard Rubin, "The Ghosts of Emmett Till," *New York Times*, July 31, 2005.

Parvez Sharma, "Chasing the American Dream in Piqua, Ohio: A Pakistani Journalist Tries to Find Refuge in Smalltown USA," *Trikone Magazine*, July 2002.

Shashi Tharoor, "Letter from America," *Newsweek International*, October 29, 2001.

Time, "As American As . . . Although Scapegoated, Muslims, Sikhs and Arabs are Patriotic, Integrated—and Growing," October 1, 2001.

Deborah Walike, "Laramie's Lessons: 'The Laramie Project' Offers Meditations on Healing and the Costs of Hatred," *Baltimore Jewish Times*, September 13, 2002.

Washington Post, "Race Was Motive for over Half the Hate Crimes in 2003, FBI Reports," November 23, 2004.

Gary Younge, "Racism Rebooted," *Nation*, July 11, 2005.

Index